GROW UP
Moving Past Spiritual Adolescence

A Flexible Inductive Study of
Ephesians

by

pam gillaspie

Scripture taken from the
NEW AMERICAN STANDARD BIBLE®,
© Copyright 1960, 1962, 1963, 1968,
1971, 1972, 1973, 1975, 1977, 1995
by The Lockman Foundation.
Used by permission. (www.Lockman.org)

Precept, Precept Ministries International,
Precept Ministries International the
Inductive Bible Study People, the Plumb
Bob design, Precept Upon Precept and
Sweeter than Chocolate are trademarks of
Precept Ministries International.

**Grow Up! Moving Past Spiritual
Adolescence**

Copyright © 2017 by Pam Gillaspie
Published by Precept Ministries
International
P.O. Box 182218
Chattanooga, Tennessee 37422
www.precept.org

ISBN 978-1-62119-615-0

Printed in the United States of America

2017

Dedicated to . . .

My Millennials. You know who you are. You are like sons and daughters to me. You know the Word of God and are not swayed by culture's lies. You are the remnant and I am blessed to minister alongside of you. Continue to grow and be strong in the Lord!

Acknowledgements

When I sit down to write the acknowledgements, I am vividly reminded that I am such a small part of the body of Christ! Thank you to my Bible study class at Immanuel Church for piloting this material with me. Thank you to my Equip Boot Camp class and fellow staffers—I had a blast studying Ephesians with you! Thank you to my family for always putting up with me and, of course, to Rick and Pete for editing and scraping off the rough edges small and great!

GROW UP
Moving Past Spiritual Adolescence
EPHESIANS

GROW UP

Moving Past Spiritual Adolescence

There is nothing quite like your favorite pair of jeans. You can dress them up, you can dress them down. You can work in them, play in them, shop in them . . . live in them. They always feel right. It is my hope that the structure of this Bible study will fit you like those jeans; that it will work with your life right now, right where you are whether you're new to this whole Bible thing or whether you've been studying the Book for years!

How is this even possible? Smoke and mirrors, perhaps? The new mercilessly thrown in the deep end? The experienced given pompoms and the job of simply cheering others on? None of the above.

Sweeter than Chocolate!® flexible studies are designed with options that will allow you to go as deep each week as you desire. If you're just starting out and feeling a little overwhelmed, stick with the main text and don't think a second thought about the sidebar assignments. If you're looking for a challenge, then take the sidebar prompts and go ahead and dig all the way to China! As you move along through the study, think of the sidebars and "Digging Deeper" boxes as that 2% of Lycra™ that you find in certain jeans . . . the wiggle room that will help them fit just right.

Beginners may find that they want to start adding in some of the optional assignments as they go along. Experts may find that when three children are throwing up for three days straight, foregoing those assignments for the week is the way to live wisely.

Life has a way of ebbing and flowing and this study is designed to ebb and flow right along with it!

Enjoy!

Contents

GROW UP
Moving Past Spiritual Adolescence
EPHESIANS

How to use this study

Sweeter than Chocolate!® studies meet you where you are and take you as far as you want to go.

1. WEEKLY STUDY: The main text guides you through the complete topic of study for the week.

2. FYI boxes: For Your Information boxes provide bite-sized material to shed additional light on the topic.

> ## FYI:
>
> **Reading Tip: Begin with prayer**
> You may have heard this a million times over and if this is a million and one, so be it. Whenever you read or study God's Word, first pray and ask His Spirit to be your Guide.

3. ONE STEP FURTHER and other sidebar boxes: Sidebar boxes give you the option to push yourself a little further. If you have extra time or are looking for an extra challenge, you can try one, all, or any number in between! These boxes give you the ultimate in flexibility.

> ## ONE STEP FURTHER:
>
> **Word Study: *torah*/law**
> The first of eight Hebrew key words we encounter for God's Word is *torah*, translated "law." If you're up for a challenge this week, do a word study to learn what you can about *torah*. Run a concordance search and examine where the word *torah* appears in the Old Testament and see what you can learn from the contexts.
>
> If you decide to look for the word for "law" in the New Testament, you'll find that the primary Greek word is *nomos*.
>
> Be sure to see what Paul says about the law in Galatians 3 and what Jesus says in Matthew 5.

4. DIGGING DEEPER boxes: If you're looking to go further, Digging Deeper sections will help you sharpen your skills as you continue to mine the truths of Scripture for yourself.

> ## Digging Deeper
>
> **What else does God's Word say about counselors?**
>
> If you can, spend some time this week digging around for what God's Word says about counselors.
>
> Start by considering what you already know about counsel from the Word of God and see if you can actually show where these truths are in the Bible. Make sure that the Word actually says what you think it says.

WEEK ONE
The Mystery!

" . . . He chose us in Him before the foundation of the world, that we would be holy and blameless before Him."
–Ephesians 1:4

Chosen. Loved. Adopted. Reconciled. Let those words sit for a moment in your mind. To be *chosen* for a team, to be *loved* by another, to be *adopted* into a family, to be *reconciled* with those you've been at odds with . . . these are powerful verbs. They touch us at our core because we were created relational beings. To discover that God Himself has chosen, loved, adopted, and reconciled us exceeds our human comprehension.

Writing to the church at Ephesus, Paul unfolds, unpacks, and flat out lavishes on his readers the truth of what it means to be in Christ and thus the object and recipient of God's ineffable love. His goodness and kindness toward those who believe is without measure! I could just keep going . . . but let's let God speak for Himself through His Word! Are you ready?!

FYI:

If You're in a Class
Begin **Week One** together on your first day of class. This will be a great way to start getting to know one another and will help those who are newer to Bible study get their bearings.

GROW UP
Moving Past Spiritual Adolescence
EPHESIANS

1

Week One: **The Mystery!**

CONSIDER the WAY you THINK

We all come to Bible study with different views and experiences. Before we get started, let's consider some of those together.

What is your view of the Bible? Do you think it is a work of man? A work of God? A little of both? Or are you not quite sure?

Do you think your view of the Bible impacts how you respond to what you read? Explain.

Do you have a background in a specific denomination or church tradition? If so, consider how that affects your reading and application of the Bible.

What is your reason for studying the Bible in general and the book of Ephesians in particular?

As we study together, it is my prayer that to the best of our ability we will drop our presuppositions and allow God's Word to speak for itself. In this we will be doing ex-egesis. Exegesis literally means "to lead out." When we deal in presuppositions and subjectivism we're falling into the trap of eisegesis (literally "to lead into")—taking the text of Scripture and tailoring it to our agendas. Eisegesis molds Scripture to fit man, but the Word accurately handled calls man to submit to the plumb line of Scripture. My goal in this class is that we will handle accurately the Word of truth and have God speak to us and change *us* through it.

FYI:

Handle the Word Accurately

Be diligent to present yourself approved to God as a workman who does not need to be ashamed, accurately handling the word of truth.

—2 Timothy 2:15

GROW UP
Moving Past Spiritual Adolescence
EPHESIANS

GETTING THE BIG PICTURE

As we begin our study together, we're going to look at the whole letter to the Ephesians, reading it through several times before we go back to examine it more thoroughly chapter by chapter. We'll start by simply reading through the letter three times this week. Use the NASB included in this Workbook for the first reading, then select two other versions of your choice.

Most Bible translations are easily accessible online if you don't have extra Bibles around the house. Try to do each read-through in a single sitting. While you may have a paraphrase version in your possession, we strongly commend a Word-For-Word version (WFW) like the NASB, ESV, or KJV.

Paraphrase translators start with the assumption that WFW versions either do not accurately translate original-language (Hebrew, Greek, Aramaic) words or, if they do, the ideas are intrinsically unclear, and so they have to either add "in-between" words or substitute new English words to explain biblical texts.

Whether or not a WFW is clear is a decision you can and should make. You'll want to use a WFW version to judge the expanded-thought text of a paraphrased version, not the other way around.

See if you can detect ideas paraphrased versions are "reading in" to the texts. And as you read, simply jot down your main observations and your biggest questions.

WEEKLY READ-THROUGH #1

Version I read: *New American Standard*

Main observations:

Big questions:

FYI:

NASB and ESV
The NASB and ESV are two reliable word-for-word translations from the original languages. While the KJV and NKJV are also translated word for word, they do not include consideration of earlier-dated original-language manuscripts discovered more recently.

FYI:

Start with Prayer
You've probably heard it before and if we study together in the future, you're sure to hear it again. Whenever you read or study God's Word, first pray and ask His Spirit to be your Guide. Jesus says that the Spirit will lead us into all truth.

GROW UP
Moving Past Spiritual Adolescence
EPHESIANS

3

Week One: **The Mystery!**

Ephesians 1

1 Paul, an apostle of Christ Jesus by the will of God, To the saints who are at Ephesus and who are faithful in Christ Jesus:

2 Grace to you and peace from God our Father and the Lord Jesus Christ.

3 Blessed be the God and Father of our Lord Jesus Christ, who has blessed us with every spiritual blessing in the heavenly places in Christ,

4 just as He chose us in Him before the foundation of the world, that we would be holy and blameless before Him. In love

5 He predestined us to adoption as sons through Jesus Christ to Himself, according to the kind intention of His will,

6 to the praise of the glory of His grace, which He freely bestowed on us in the Beloved.

7 In Him we have redemption through His blood, the forgiveness of our trespasses, according to the riches of His grace

8 which He lavished on us. In all wisdom and insight

9 He made known to us the mystery of His will, according to His kind intention which He purposed in Him

10 with a view to an administration suitable to the fullness of the times, that is, the summing up of all things in Christ, things in the heavens and things on the earth. In Him

11 also we have obtained an inheritance, having been predestined according to His purpose who works all things after the counsel of His will,

12 to the end that we who were the first to hope in Christ would be to the praise of His glory.

13 In Him, you also, after listening to the message of truth, the gospel of your salvation—having also believed, you were sealed in Him with the Holy Spirit of promise,

14 who is given as a pledge of our inheritance, with a view to the redemption of God's own possession, to the praise of His glory.

15 For this reason I too, having heard of the faith in the Lord Jesus which exists among you and your love for all the saints,

16 do not cease giving thanks for you, while making mention of you in my prayers;

17 that the God of our Lord Jesus Christ, the Father of glory, may give to you a spirit of wisdom and of revelation in the knowledge of Him.

18 I pray that the eyes of your heart may be enlightened, so that you will know what is the hope of His calling, what are the riches of the glory of His inheritance in the saints,

19 and what is the surpassing greatness of His power toward us who believe. These are in accordance with the working of the strength of His might

20 which He brought about in Christ, when He raised Him from the dead and seated Him at His right hand in the heavenly places,

---

FYI:

Key Words

Identifying key words helps us discover the author's main point or points. Key words are often repeated and are "key" to unlocking a text's meaning.

KEY WORDS:

Ephesians 1

As you read, jot down repeated words and phrases that you notice. As we overview, only mark down things that jump off the page at you. We'll have the next several weeks to immerse ourselves in the details.

GROW UP
Moving Past Spiritual Adolescence
EPHESIANS

21 far above all rule and authority and power and dominion, and every name that is named, not only in this age but also in the one to come.

22 And He put all things in subjection under His feet, and gave Him as head over all things to the church,

23 which is His body, the fullness of Him who fills all in all.

Ephesians 2

1 And you were dead in your trespasses and sins,

2 in which you formerly walked according to the course of this world, according to the prince of the power of the air, of the spirit that is now working in the sons of disobedience.

3 Among them we too all formerly lived in the lusts of our flesh, indulging the desires of the flesh and of the mind, and were by nature children of wrath, even as the rest.

4 But God, being rich in mercy, because of His great love with which He loved us,

5 even when we were dead in our transgressions, made us alive together with Christ (by grace you have been saved),

6 and raised us up with Him, and seated us with Him in the heavenly places in Christ Jesus,

7 so that in the ages to come He might show the surpassing riches of His grace in kindness toward us in Christ Jesus.

8 For by grace you have been saved through faith; and that not of yourselves, it is the gift of God;

9 not as a result of works, so that no one may boast.

10 For we are His workmanship, created in Christ Jesus for good works, which God prepared beforehand so that we would walk in them.

11 Therefore remember that formerly you, the Gentiles in the flesh, who are called "Uncircumcision" by the so-called "Circumcision," which is performed in the flesh by human hands—

12 remember that you were at that time separate from Christ, excluded from the commonwealth of Israel, and strangers to the covenants of promise, having no hope and without God in the world.

13 But now in Christ Jesus you who formerly were far off have been brought near by the blood of Christ.

14 For He Himself is our peace, who made both groups into one and broke down the barrier of the dividing wall,

15 by abolishing in His flesh the enmity, which is the Law of commandments contained in ordinances, so that in Himself He might make the two into one new man, thus establishing peace,

16 and might reconcile them both in one body to God through the cross, by it having put to death the enmity.

KEY WORDS:

Ephesians 2
As you read, jot down repeated words and phrases that you notice.

GROW UP
Moving Past Spiritual Adolescence
EPHESIANS

Week One: **The Mystery!**

17 *AND HE CAME AND PREACHED PEACE TO YOU WHO WERE FAR AWAY, AND PEACE TO THOSE WHO WERE NEAR;*

18 *for through Him we both have our access in one Spirit to the Father.*

19 *So then you are no longer strangers and aliens, but you are fellow citizens with the saints, and are of God's household,*

20 *having been built on the foundation of the apostles and prophets, Christ Jesus Himself being the corner stone,*

21 *in whom the whole building, being fitted together, is growing into a holy temple in the Lord,*

22 *in whom you also are being built together into a dwelling of God in the Spirit.*

Ephesians 3

1 *For this reason I, Paul, the prisoner of Christ Jesus for the sake of you Gentiles—*

2 *if indeed you have heard of the stewardship of God's grace which was given to me for you;*

3 *that by revelation there was made known to me the mystery, as I wrote before in brief.*

4 *By referring to this, when you read you can understand my insight into the mystery of Christ,*

5 *which in other generations was not made known to the sons of men, as it has now been revealed to His holy apostles and prophets in the Spirit;*

6 *to be specific, that the Gentiles are fellow heirs and fellow members of the body, and fellow partakers of the promise in Christ Jesus through the gospel,*

7 *of which I was made a minister, according to the gift of God's grace which was given to me according to the working of His power.*

8 *To me, the very least of all saints, this grace was given, to preach to the Gentiles the unfathomable riches of Christ,*

9 *and to bring to light what is the administration of the mystery which for ages has been hidden in God who created all things;*

10 *so that the manifold wisdom of God might now be made known through the church to the rulers and the authorities in the heavenly places.*

11 *This was in accordance with the eternal purpose which He carried out in Christ Jesus our Lord,*

12 *in whom we have boldness and confident access through faith in Him.*

13 *Therefore I ask you not to lose heart at my tribulations on your behalf, for they are your glory.*

14 *For this reason I bow my knees before the Father,*

15 *from whom every family in heaven and on earth derives its name,*

16 *that He would grant you, according to the riches of His glory, to be strengthened with power through His Spirit in the inner man,*

KEY WORDS:

Ephesians 3
Jot down repeated words and phrases that you notice.

GROW UP
Moving Past Spiritual Adolescence
EPHESIANS

17 so that Christ may dwell in your hearts through faith; and *that you, being rooted and grounded in love,*

18 may be able to comprehend with all the saints what is the breadth and length and height and depth,

19 and to know the love of Christ which surpasses knowledge, that you may be filled up to all the fullness of God.

20 Now to Him who is able to do far more abundantly beyond all that we ask or think, according to the power that works within us,

21 to Him be the glory in the church and in Christ Jesus to all generations forever and ever. Amen.

Ephesians 4

1 Therefore I, the prisoner of the Lord, implore you to walk in a manner worthy of the calling with which you have been called,

2 with all humility and gentleness, with patience, showing tolerance for one another in love,

3 being diligent to preserve the unity of the Spirit in the bond of peace.

4 There is one body and one Spirit, just as also you were called in one hope of your calling;

5 one Lord, one faith, one baptism,

6 one God and Father of all who is over all and through all and in all.

7 But to each one of us grace was given according to the measure of Christ's gift.

8 Therefore it says, "WHEN HE ASCENDED ON HIGH, HE LED CAPTIVE A HOST OF CAPTIVES, AND HE GAVE GIFTS TO MEN."

9 (Now this expression, "He ascended," what does it mean except that He also had descended into the lower parts of the earth?

10 He who descended is Himself also He who ascended far above all the heavens, so that He might fill all things.)

11 And He gave some as apostles, and some as prophets, and some as evangelists, and some as pastors and teachers,

12 for the equipping of the saints for the work of service, to the building up of the body of Christ;

13 until we all attain to the unity of the faith, and of the knowledge of the Son of God, to a mature man, to the measure of the stature which belongs to the fullness of Christ.

14 As a result, we are no longer to be children, tossed here and there by waves and carried about by every wind of doctrine, by the trickery of men, by craftiness in deceitful scheming;

15 but speaking the truth in love, we are to grow up in all aspects into Him who is the head, even Christ,

KEY WORDS:

Ephesians 4
Continue to jot down repeated words and phrases that you notice. This should be getting easier! Is it?

GROW UP
Moving Past Spiritual Adolescence
EPHESIANS

Week One: **The Mystery!**

16 from whom the whole body, being fitted and held together by what every joint supplies, according to the proper working of each individual part, causes the growth of the body for the building up of itself in love.

17 So this I say, and affirm together with the Lord, that you walk no longer just as the Gentiles also walk, in the futility of their mind,

18 being darkened in their understanding, excluded from the life of God because of the ignorance that is in them, because of the hardness of their heart;

19 and they, having become callous, have given themselves over to sensuality for the practice of every kind of impurity with greediness.

20 But you did not learn Christ in this way,

21 if indeed you have heard Him and have been taught in Him, just as truth is in Jesus,

22 that, in reference to your former manner of life, you lay aside the old self, which is being corrupted in accordance with the lusts of deceit,

23 and that you be renewed in the spirit of your mind,

24 and put on the new self, which in the likeness of God has been created in righteousness and holiness of the truth.

25 Therefore, laying aside falsehood, SPEAK TRUTH EACH ONE of you WITH HIS NEIGHBOR, for we are members of one another.

26 BE ANGRY, AND yet DO NOT SIN; do not let the sun go down on your anger,

27 and do not give the devil an opportunity.

28 He who steals must steal no longer; but rather he must labor, performing with his own hands what is good, so that he will have something to share with one who has need.

29 Let no unwholesome word proceed from your mouth, but only such a word as is good for edification according to the need of the moment, so that it will give grace to those who hear.

30 Do not grieve the Holy Spirit of God, by whom you were sealed for the day of redemption.

31 Let all bitterness and wrath and anger and clamor and slander be put away from you, along with all malice.

32 Be kind to one another, tender-hearted, forgiving each other, just as God in Christ also has forgiven you.

Ephesians 5

1 Therefore be imitators of God, as beloved children;

2 and walk in love, just as Christ also loved you and gave Himself up for us, an offering and a sacrifice to God as a fragrant aroma.

3 But immorality or any impurity or greed must not even be named among you, as is proper among saints;

4 and there must be no filthiness and silly talk, or coarse jesting, which are not fitting, but rather giving of thanks.

5   For this you know with certainty, that no immoral or impure person or covetous man, who is an idolater, has an inheritance in the kingdom of Christ and God.

6   Let no one deceive you with empty words, for because of these things the wrath of God comes upon the sons of disobedience.

7   Therefore do not be partakers with them;

8   for you were formerly darkness, but now you are Light in the Lord; walk as children of Light

9   (for the fruit of the Light consists in all goodness and righteousness and truth),

10 trying to learn what is pleasing to the Lord.

11 Do not participate in the unfruitful deeds of darkness, but instead even expose them;

12 for it is disgraceful even to speak of the things which are done by them in secret.

13 But all things become visible when they are exposed by the light, for everything that becomes visible is light.

14 For this reason it says, "Awake, sleeper, and arise from the dead, and Christ will shine on you."

15 Therefore be careful how you walk, not as unwise men but as wise,

16 making the most of your time, because the days are evil.

17 So then do not be foolish, but understand what the will of the Lord is.

18 And do not get drunk with wine, for that is dissipation, but be filled with the Spirit,

19 speaking to one another in psalms and hymns and spiritual songs, singing and making melody with your heart to the Lord;

20 always giving thanks for all things in the name of our Lord Jesus Christ to God, even the Father;

21 and be subject to one another in the fear of Christ.

22 Wives, be subject to your own husbands, as to the Lord.

23 For the husband is the head of the wife, as Christ also is the head of the church, He Himself being the Savior of the body.

24 But as the church is subject to Christ, so also the wives ought to be to their husbands in everything.

25 Husbands, love your wives, just as Christ also loved the church and gave Himself up for her,

26 so that He might sanctify her, having cleansed her by the washing of water with the word,

27 that He might present to Himself the church in all her glory, having no spot or wrinkle or any such thing; but that she would be holy and blameless.

28 So husbands ought also to love their own wives as their own bodies. He who loves his own wife loves himself;

KEY WORDS:

Ephesians 5
Jot down key words and repeated phrases.

GROW UP
Moving Past Spiritual Adolescence
EPHESIANS

Week One: **The Mystery!**

29 for no one ever hated his own flesh, but nourishes and cherishes it, just as Christ also does the church,

30 because we are members of His body.

31 FOR THIS REASON A MAN SHALL LEAVE HIS FATHER AND MOTHER AND SHALL BE JOINED TO HIS WIFE, AND THE TWO SHALL BECOME ONE FLESH.

32 This mystery is great; but I am speaking with reference to Christ and the church.

33 Nevertheless, each individual among you also is to love his own wife even as himself, and the wife must see to it that she respects her husband.

Ephesians 6

1 Children, obey your parents in the Lord, for this is right.

2 HONOR YOUR FATHER AND MOTHER (which is the first commandment with a promise),

3 SO THAT IT MAY BE WELL WITH YOU, AND THAT YOU MAY LIVE LONG ON THE EARTH.

4 Fathers, do not provoke your children to anger, but bring them up in the discipline and instruction of the Lord.

5 Slaves, be obedient to those who are your masters according to the flesh, with fear and trembling, in the sincerity of your heart, as to Christ;

6 not by way of eyeservice, as men-pleasers, but as slaves of Christ, doing the will of God from the heart.

7 With good will render service, as to the Lord, and not to men,

8 knowing that whatever good thing each one does, this he will receive back from the Lord, whether slave or free.

9 And masters, do the same things to them, and give up threatening, knowing that both their Master and yours is in heaven, and there is no partiality with Him.

10 Finally, be strong in the Lord and in the strength of His might.

11 Put on the full armor of God, so that you will be able to stand firm against the schemes of the devil.

12 For our struggle is not against flesh and blood, but against the rulers, against the powers, against the world forces of this darkness, against the spiritual forces of wickedness in the heavenly places.

13 Therefore, take up the full armor of God, so that you will be able to resist in the evil day, and having done everything, to stand firm.

14 Stand firm therefore, HAVING GIRDED YOUR LOINS WITH TRUTH, and HAVING PUT ON THE BREASTPLATE OF RIGHTEOUSNESS,

15 and having shod YOUR FEET WITH THE PREPARATION OF THE GOSPEL OF PEACE;

16 in addition to all, taking up the shield of faith with which you will be able to extinguish all the flaming arrows of the evil one.

KEY WORDS:

Ephesians 6

You're pretty close to "professional" by now! Finish strong by jotting down the key words and phrases you've observed in Ephesians 6.

GROW UP

Moving Past Spiritual Adolescence
EPHESIANS

17   And take THE HELMET OF SALVATION, and the sword of the Spirit, which is the word of God.

18   With all prayer and petition pray at all times in the Spirit, and with this in view, be on the alert with all perseverance and petition for all the saints,

19   and pray on my behalf, that utterance may be given to me in the opening of my mouth, to make known with boldness the mystery of the gospel,

20   for which I am an ambassador in chains; that in proclaiming it I may speak boldly, as I ought to speak.

21   But that you also may know about my circumstances, how I am doing, Tychicus, the beloved brother and faithful minister in the Lord, will make everything known to you.

22   I have sent him to you for this very purpose, so that you may know about us, and that he may comfort your hearts.

23   Peace be to the brethren, and love with faith, from God the Father and the Lord Jesus Christ.

24   Grace be with all those who love our Lord Jesus Christ with incorruptible love.

WEEKLY READ-THROUGH #2

Version I read:

Main observations:

Big questions:

GROW UP
Moving Past Spiritual Adolescence
EPHESIANS

ONE STEP FURTHER:

What are you bringing to the text?

We've already talked about general presuppositions we bring to the Bible, but now that you've read the text, it would be good to revisit any you may have missed that relate to the content of this specific letter. I'll start you off with a few hot topics and you can complete the list with others. What presuppositions do you bring with regard to:

• Marriage

• God's will/purpose

• The Church

• Spiritual gifts

•

•

•

•

•

•

Week One: **The Mystery!**

WEEKLY READ-THROUGH #3

Version I read:

Main observations:

Big questions:

DISCUSS with your GROUP or PONDER on your own . . .

As you read, were you aware of any presuppositions you brought to the text? Do you have views that predisposed you toward a particular interpretation? If so, make note of them.

What differences did you notice between the translations?

If you used a paraphrase, what differences did you notice with it?

WHO, WHAT, WHEN, WHERE, WHY, and HOW

Who wrote Ephesians? Who was he writing to? (author and recipients)

What kind of writing is this? (genre)

Approximately when do you think Ephesians was written? What timing clues did you see?

Where was the author writing from (origin)? Can we know for certain? Why/why not?

Where were the recipients located (destination)? What were they like? How does Paul describe them?

Why did Paul write the Ephesians (occasion)?

GROW UP
Moving Past Spiritual Adolescence
EPHESIANS

EPHESUS ELSEWHERE IN THE BIBLE

Having read through Ephesians at least three times this week, you've seen for your-self that the believers there were a faithful bunch. Unlike many other New Testament letters that address some serious junk going on in churches, Ephesians doesn't.

Whether the letter was written to a specific church or to a group of churches in the region of Ephesus, the internal evidence points to a group of people who, for the most part, had their collective act together.

Before we call it a week, let's look at the last mention of the Ephesian church in Scripture as it is a cautionary word we'll want to keep in mind as we study.

OBSERVE the TEXT of SCRIPTURE

Jesus addresses seven churches in the book of Revelation. The first of these churches was located in Ephesus. From the first chapter (1:1, 12-16) we can infer that the speaker is Jesus.

READ Revelation 2:1-7 and **MARK** every reference to *Jesus*. Next, **MARK** every refer-ence to the *church in Ephesus* (be sure to include pronouns). Finally, **MARK** every occurrence of *deeds*.

Revelation 2:1-7

1 *"To the angel of the church in Ephesus write:*

The One who holds the seven stars in His right hand, the One who walks among the seven golden lampstands, says this:

2 *'I know your deeds and your toil and perseverance, and that you cannot tolerate evil men, and you put to the test those who call themselves apostles, and they are not, and you found them to be false;*

3 *and you have perseverance and have endured for My name's sake, and have not grown weary.*

4 *'But I have this against you, that you have left your first love.*

5 *'Therefore remember from where you have fallen, and repent and do the deeds you did at first; or else I am coming to you and will remove your lampstand out of its place—unless you repent.*

6 *'Yet this you do have, that you hate the deeds of the Nicolaitans, which I also hate.*

7 *'He who has an ear, let him hear what the Spirit says to the churches. To him who overcomes, I will grant to eat of the tree of life which is in the Paradise of God.'*

DISCUSS with your GROUP or PONDER on your own . . .

Let's start out by looking at Jesus. Summarize in a short paragraph or list what you learned about Him in this text.

According to verses 2 and 3, what does Jesus say He knows about the Ephesian church?

Based on these verses, what kind of threats do you think had come against them?

What action(s) did they take in the face of the threats and why?

What does Jesus have *against* them? What three actions does He call them to do in response?

According to verse 6, what does Jesus have in common with the Ephesian church?

Compare the usages of the term *deeds* in verses 2, 5, and 6.

How do you think the difference in the deeds of verses 2 and 5 relates to the Ephesians' abandonment of their first love?

@THE END OF THE DAY . . .

I hope you've enjoyed reading and rereading the letter to the Ephesians this week. There is perhaps no better way to study the text of Scripture than to simply read and reread carefully, asking questions along the way. That said, remember as we move forward in our study that this Workbook is designed to help you get into God's Book and learn to ask good questions; it is never supposed to be a replacement. When the weeks get busy and the calendar boxes aren't big enough to hold all of the day's events, remember that God's Book always trumps a workbook! Always!

Before you call it a day, take a few minutes to think and pray through what you've studied this week. Then, write down your one biggest takeaway. Yup, only one for now. We'll get to more later!

WEEK TWO
God's Kind Intention Toward You!

*"In Him, you also, after listening to the message of truth,
the gospel of your salvation–having also believed, you were
sealed in Him with the Holy Spirit of promise . . . "*
–Ephesians 1:13

How often do people live in fear and trembling at the idea of "the will of God" as though a distant God is out to get them and make their lives miserable? The thinking can go something like this: *If I fully surrender to God's will, He will send me as a missionary to the middle of nowhere where I will be "in His will" but miserable. If I fully surrender to God's will, He'll hurt someone I love to give me a "powerful testimony." If I fully surrender to God's will, heaven awaits but earth will be hell.* You've probably heard forms of this thinking. You may have heard it in your own head!

This thinking grows from a perverted and distorted view of God and His intentions towards those He loves. Will the Christian life be butterflies and rainbows with Jesus at the helm? Of course not. It may be taught in some churches, but it isn't biblical Christianity. Jesus Himself assured His disciples that they would have tribulation: "In the world you have tribulation, but take courage; I have overcome the world" (John 16:33b). Life in a broken and fallen world is hard, but take heart, my friends; if you are in relationship with God through Jesus Christ, the intention of God's will toward you is kind! That is life-giving news!

Week Two: **God's Kind Intention Toward You!**

REMEMBERING

Take a few minutes to summarize what you learned last week.

INDUCTIVE FOCUS:

Questioning the Text

The key to exegesis (the fancy word for discovering what Scripture says) is questioning the text. As we do this, we'll use the basic investigative questions *Who? What? When? Where? Why?* and *How?* as we read. As we study God's Word together, realize there's a limit to the number of questions I can ask from week to week in a workbook format. If I ask too many, people will run away screaming! That said, don't let inherent limitations of a class stop you from asking other questions and exploring further on your own! We will never run out of questions to ask and answers to glean from God's Word!

If you're at a loss for what questions to ask, pay attention to the words that you've marked. Go to your key words and start there with your questions! Marking helps you see the main idea and frame questions.

WEEKLY READ-THROUGH #1

Let's begin by reading through the text in three different versions as we did last week. We'll continue to do this each week. You can't read the text too much!

Version I read:

New observations/questions:

WEEKLY READ-THROUGH #2

Version I read:

New observations/questions:

WEEKLY READ-THROUGH #3

Version I read:

New observations/questions:

EPHESIANS 1

Paul opens his letter to the Ephesians with the familiar greeting "Paul, an apostle of Christ Jesus," but then takes a different tack from what he does with most of his letters. Let's take a look.

OBSERVE the TEXT of SCRIPTURE

READ Ephesians 1 and **MARK** key, repeated words in a distinctive fashion.

Ephesians 1

1 *Paul, an apostle of Christ Jesus by the will of God,*
   To the saints who are at Ephesus and who are faithful in Christ Jesus:

2 *Grace to you and peace from God our Father and the Lord Jesus Christ.*

3 *Blessed be the God and Father of our Lord Jesus Christ, who has blessed us with every spiritual blessing in the heavenly places in Christ,*

4 *just as He chose us in Him before the foundation of the world, that we would be holy and blameless before Him. In love*

5 *He predestined us to adoption as sons through Jesus Christ to Himself, according to the kind intention of His will,*

6 *to the praise of the glory of His grace, which He freely bestowed on us in the Beloved.*

7 *In Him we have redemption through His blood, the forgiveness of our trespasses, according to the riches of His grace*

8 *which He lavished on us. In all wisdom and insight*

9 *He made known to us the mystery of His will, according to His kind intention which He purposed in Him*

> **FYI:**
>
> **Marking the Text**
> You'll find some key words to mark on the following pages, but it's better for everyone—and loads more fun for you!—if you can begin identifying them for yourself.

GROW UP
Moving Past Spiritual Adolescence
EPHESIANS

Notes

10 *with a view to an administration suitable to the fullness of the times,* that is, *the summing up of all things in Christ, things in the heavens and things on the earth. In Him*

11 *also we have obtained an inheritance, having been predestined according to His purpose who works all things after the counsel of His will,*

12 *to the end that we who were the first to hope in Christ would be to the praise of His glory.*

13 *In Him, you also, after listening to the message of truth, the gospel of your salvation—having also believed, you were sealed in Him with the Holy Spirit of promise,*

14 *who is given as a pledge of our inheritance, with a view to the redemption of God's own possession, to the praise of His glory.*

15 *For this reason I too, having heard of the faith in the Lord Jesus which exists among you and your love for all the saints,*

16 *do not cease giving thanks for you, while making mention of you in my prayers;*

17 *that the God of our Lord Jesus Christ, the Father of glory, may give to you a spirit of wisdom and of revelation in the knowledge of Him.*

18 *I pray that the eyes of your heart may be enlightened, so that you will know what is the hope of His calling, what are the riches of the glory of His inheritance in the saints,*

19 *and what is the surpassing greatness of His power toward us who believe. These are in accordance with the working of the strength of His might*

20 *which He brought about in Christ, when He raised Him from the dead and seated Him at His right hand in the heavenly places,*

21 *far above all rule and authority and power and dominion, and every name that is named, not only in this age but also in the one to come.*

22 *And He put all things in subjection under His feet, and gave Him as head over all things to the church,*

23 *which is His body, the fullness of Him who fills all in all.*

DISCUSS with your GROUP or PONDER on your own . . .

What did you initially observe from the text?

GROW UP

Moving Past Spiritual Adolescence
EPHESIANS

What key words and/or phrases did you notice?

Briefly summarize Ephesians 1.

LOOKING CLOSER . . .
OBSERVE the TEXT of SCRIPTURE

READ Ephesians 1:1-2 and **MARK** every reference to the letter's author and recipients (be sure to include pronouns).

Ephesians 1:1-2

1 *Paul, an apostle of Christ Jesus by the will of God,*

   To the saints who are at Ephesus and who are faithful in Christ Jesus:

2 *Grace to you and peace from God our Father and the Lord Jesus Christ.*

DISCUSS with your GROUP or PONDER on your own . . .

Who is the author? Briefly describe him.

Did he choose his position? Do you think this matters? Why/why not?

ONE STEP FURTHER:

How Does It Differ?
If you have some extra time this week, review the opening chapters of Paul's other letters to see how Ephesians compares. What is similar? What is different? Then, record your observations below.

FYI:

Charis and Shalom
"Grace [Greek: *charis*] and peace [Greek: *eirene*/Hebrew: *shalom*]" merge a typical Greek greeting with a common Jewish one.

GROW UP
Moving Past Spiritual Adolescence
EPHESIANS

Week Two: **God's Kind Intention Toward You!**

Describe the recipients.

What do the author and recipients have in common?

What truths about God did you observe in these verses?

INDUCTIVE FOCUS:

Important Words/Word Groups and Phrases in Ephesians 1

Here are some words and word groups to pay attention to in Ephesians 1.

"God" words (*God, Father, Jesus Christ, Lord,* etc.)

"Will" words (*will, purpose, intention*)

"Choice" words (*chose, predestined*)

"Power" words (*power, strength, might*)

"Knowledge" words (*knowledge, know, made known*)

"Inheritance" words (*inheritance, heir*)

"Faith/believe"

"Grace"

Here are some critical phrases to watch for:

"in Christ"

"to the praise of His glory"

"according to . . ."

Jot down any other significant words or phrases you noticed.

OBSERVE the TEXT of SCRIPTURE

Paul pours out a dose of dense theology in verses 3-14 that gives us a glimpse into the will and purpose of God, how that relates to us, and how He accomplishes His work in us—we who are in Christ. Let's take a look!

READ Ephesians 1:3-14 and **MARK** references to *God* and to *God's will* (*will, purpose, intention*) and occurrences of *in Christ* including synonyms. Then go back and **CIRCLE** every reference to *us/we*.

Ephesians 1:3-14

3 Blessed be *the God and Father of our Lord Jesus Christ, who has blessed us with every spiritual blessing in the heavenly places in Christ,*

4 *just as He chose us in Him before the foundation of the world, that we would be holy and blameless before Him. In love*

5 *He predestined us to adoption as sons through Jesus Christ to Himself, according to the kind intention of His will,*

6 *to the praise of the glory of His grace, which He freely bestowed on us in the Beloved.*

7 *In Him we have redemption through His blood, the forgiveness of our trespasses, according to the riches of His grace*

8 *which He lavished on us. In all wisdom and insight*

9 *He made known to us the mystery of His will, according to His kind intention which He purposed in Him*

10 *with a view to an administration suitable to the fullness of the times, that is, the summing up of all things in Christ, things in the heavens and things on the earth. In Him*

11 *also we have obtained an inheritance, having been predestined according to His purpose who works all things after the counsel of His will,*

12 *to the end that we who were the first to hope in Christ would be to the praise of His glory.*

13 *In Him, you also, after listening to the message of truth, the gospel of your salvation—having also believed, you were sealed in Him with the Holy Spirit of promise,*

14 *who is given as a pledge of our inheritance, with a view to the redemption of God's own* possession, *to the praise of His glory.*

DISCUSS with your GROUP or PONDER on your own . . .

How does Paul describe God in verse 3? What does he say about the Father? About Jesus?

Looking at verses 3-6, what did God do for us "before the foundation of the world"? What implications do these have? (Follow the verb trail!)

According to verse 4, when did God choose "us" and "in whom"? What does this imply about our salvation? What did He choose us to be before Him?

According to verses 5-6, what did God predestine "us" to and how? What does Jesus have to do with this? How is this related to the inheritance mentioned in verse 11? What does this give to God?

FYI:

One Long Sentence
Believe it or not, Ephesians 1:3-14 is one loooooong sentence in Greek. If you're wondering why it is a little hard to follow, it's because . . . it's a little hard to follow!

Don't think, though, that it is inferior writing or unintelligible; lengthy sentences are not uncommon in Greek prose. If you're having a hard time following Paul's train of thought, simply slow down and watch the grammar closely.

FYI:

Saints
"Holy" comes from the Greek *hagios* (set apart). It is also translated as "saint."

GROW UP
Moving Past Spiritual Adolescence
EPHESIANS

23

If your salvation results from God's choice rather than your behavior, what affect should this have on your ego? Explain.

ONE STEP FURTHER:

Word Studies

If you have time this week, see what you can discover about the Greek words that are translated "chose" and "predestined." You'll want to see where and how they are used elsewhere in Paul's writings and in the rest of the New Testament. Then record what you learn below.

Chose

Predestined

Describe God's grace according to verses 5-8. How and in what measure does God give it?

According to verses 7-12, what are some of the benefits we have from God? What difference does each make in life? What difference has each made in *your* life?

What specifically do we have through Christ's blood? Why do we need this? What does it have to do with everything else?

What did God make known to believers according to verses 9 and 10? How would you explain this?

GROW UP
Moving Past Spiritual Adolescence
EPHESIANS

When were we sealed by the Holy Spirit according to verse 13? What assurance of "our inheritance" do we have?

Looking back at where you marked references to God's will (*will, purpose, intention*), make a list summarizing what you marked.

One key phrase throughout Paul's writings, particularly here in Ephesians, is "in Christ." List everything the text says about being "in Christ." Then, note what this has to do with God's actions toward us.

By way of summary, how would you explain to someone else what God's disposition towards you is and what He has done for you in Christ?

How can these truths about God's kind intention (Greek: *eudokia*) hold you during difficult times?

How can the truths you've learned about the benefits of being "in Christ" affect the way you walk with Him day by day?

ONE STEP FURTHER:

Word Studies

Here are a few more words to explore if you have the time and energy! Blueletterbible.org is a great resource for exploring biblical words in the original languages of Greek, Hebrew, and Aramaic.

Purpose

Will

Kind Intention

GROW UP

Moving Past Spiritual Adolescence
EPHESIANS

Digging Deeper

Acts 18–20: Where Ephesians "Fits"

If you want to discover more about the Ephesians firsthand from the book of Acts, spend some time in Acts 18–20 this week. Acts 18 opens with Paul leaving Athens, going to Corinth, and there meeting Aquila and Priscilla, husband-wife refugees from Rome.

Acts 18

How long does Paul stay in Corinth?

Who does Paul leave in Ephesus on his way to Syria? What does he do while he is there? What does he tell them as he leaves?

Who arrives in Ephesus in Acts 18:24? What is he like? What interaction do Priscilla and Aquila have with him and why?

Acts 19

What does Paul find when he first returns to Ephesus? What happens?

What does Paul do for the first three months while at Ephesus? How do the people in the city respond?

GROW UP

Moving Past Spiritual Adolescence
EPHESIANS

What does he do for the next two years and what results?

What else does God do through Paul at Ephesus? What happens?

How do people respond to the name of the Lord Jesus according to Acts 19:17?

What happens with regard to "the word of the Lord" according to Acts 19:20?

Briefly summarize the row that takes place when Demetrius the silversmith stirs up the people. What does this tell us about the city at large?

Acts 20

Where does Paul go after the riot calms? Does he ever make it back to Ephesus? Why/why not?

Where does Paul meet with the elders of Ephesus?

What does he want to tell them?

What does he warn them about?

How does this compare with what we looked at in Revelation 2 last week?

Summarize additional information you learned from Acts:

• about Ephesus

• about the Ephesians

• about Paul's heart for and warnings to them

OBSERVE the TEXT of SCRIPTURE

READ Ephesians 1:15-23 and **MARK** references to the recipients (in this case it will be mainly second person pronouns—*you, your*, etc.). **UNDERLINE** what Paul prays for them.

Ephesians 1:15-23

15 For this reason I too, having heard of the faith in the Lord Jesus which exists among you and your love for all the saints,

16 do not cease giving thanks for you, while making mention of you *in my prayers;*

17 that the God of our Lord Jesus Christ, the Father of glory, may give to you a spirit of wisdom and of revelation in the knowledge of Him.

18 I pray that the eyes of your heart may be enlightened, so that you will know what is the hope of His calling, what are the riches of the glory of His inheritance in the saints,

19 and what is the surpassing greatness of His power toward us who believe. These are in accordance with the working of the strength of His might

20 which He brought about in Christ, when He raised Him from the dead and seated Him at His right hand in the heavenly places,

21 far above all rule and authority and power and dominion, and every name that is named, not only in this age but also in the one to come.

22 And He put all things in subjection under His feet, and gave Him as head over all things to the church,

23 which is His body, the fullness of Him who fills all in all.

DISCUSS with your GROUP or PONDER on your own . . .

What is the reason that Paul does not cease giving thanks for his readers?

What else do we learn about the recipients in this section?

ONE STEP FURTHER:

Other Prayers

The best place we can learn how to pray and what to pray is from God's Word itself. This week, if you have some extra time, see what other examples of prayer you can find in the pages of Scripture and record what you learn below.

GROW UP

Moving Past Spiritual Adolescence
EPHESIANS

Week Two: **God's Kind Intention Toward You!**

What does Paul want for them and pray that God will give them? (Yes, it's a list!)

What are the spirit of wisdom and of revelation anchored in?

Where does knowledge of Christ come from?

What specifically does Paul pray they will *know*?

What can we learn about praying from this example? As you answer, think for a moment about how Paul's prayer compares with those you typically pray or hear prayed.

How does Paul further describe the greatness of God's power toward believers? What else did this power do in history?

If that kind of power is at work in your life, is there anything God wants us to do that is impossible? Explain. How effective will this power be for living righteously? For overcoming sin?

FYI:

Nothing Is Impossible
And Jesus said to His disciples, "Truly I say to you, it is hard for a rich man to enter the kingdom of heaven. Again I say to you, it is easier for a camel to go through the eye of a needle, than for a rich man to enter the kingdom of God." When the disciples heard this, they were very astonished and said, "Then who can be saved?" And looking at them Jesus said to them, "With people this is impossible, but with God all things are possible."

—Matthew 19:23-26

What superlative words in this section describe the position and authority of Jesus Christ?

What else do we learn about God in this section?

What specifically is the relationship of Christ to the Church and vice versa? What response do you think this should elicit in believers? Are you living in light of this truth?

GROW UP
Moving Past Spiritual Adolescence
EPHESIANS

@THE END OF THE DAY . . .

As you think back through what we've learned this past week, try to summarize the chapter as a hashtag. Then write a little longer summary (a status or tweet length). Finally, prayerfully consider how you will apply what you've learned from God's Word this week.

Ephesians 1

Hashtag #:

One-Sentence Summary:

My Application(s):

WEEK THREE
The Walking Dead

"And you were dead in your trespasses and sins, in which you formerly walked . . ."
–Ephesians 2:1-2a

Like it or not, zombies are all the rage in pop culture. The "undead" terrify those looking for adrenaline-fueled viewing options on the big screen and the small screen alike. They also dominate the world of video games as young males in particular gear up with virtual weapons to save the world from a zombie apocalypse. We've become so accustomed to zombies as fictional entertainment that it's easy to become calloused to the fact that, theologically speaking, the world today is filled with legions of the "living" dead. Thousands of years before Stephen King, Paul wrote to the Ephesians about them. Let's take a look!

Notes

REMEMBERING

Take a few minutes to summarize what you learned last week.

What truth have you been most actively applying?

WEEKLY READ-THROUGH #1

Version I read:

New observations/questions:

WEEKLY READ-THROUGH #2

Version I read:

New observations/questions:

ONE STEP FURTHER:

What prison?
If you have some extra time this week, see what you can discover about Paul's various imprisonments. Use whatever resources you need: a concordance, a Bible dictionary, commentaries, etc. Then, explain where you think he was when he penned the letter to the Ephesians. Be sure to cite your references!

GROW UP
Moving Past Spiritual Adolescence
EPHESIANS

Notes

WEEKLY READ-THROUGH #3

Version I read:

New observations/questions:

FYI:

We're reading Ephesians again?
Your most important study time will be reading Ephesians carefully on your own. I know it's tempting to skip over read-it-again instructions, but there is no better investment of your time than abiding in the pure Word of God!

EPHESIANS 2

While Ephesians 1 unfolds the beauty and riches of being in Christ, Ephesians 2 opens with a reminder of how terrible our condition used to be.

OBSERVE the TEXT of SCRIPTURE

READ Ephesians 2 and **MARK** key, repeated words in a distinctive fashion.

Ephesians 2

1 *And you were dead in your trespasses and sins,*

2 *in which you formerly walked according to the course of this world, according to the prince of the power of the air, of the spirit that is now working in the sons of disobedience.*

3 *Among them we too all formerly lived in the lusts of our flesh, indulging the desires of the flesh and of the mind, and were by nature children of wrath, even as the rest.*

4 *But God, being rich in mercy, because of His great love with which He loved us,*

5 *even when we were dead in our transgressions, made us alive together with Christ (by grace you have been saved),*

6 *and raised us up with Him, and seated us with Him in the heavenly* places *in Christ Jesus,*

7 *so that in the ages to come He might show the surpassing riches of His grace in kindness toward us in Christ Jesus.*

8 *For by grace you have been saved through faith; and that not of yourselves,* it is *the gift of God;*

9 *not as a result of works, so that no one may boast.*

10 *For we are His workmanship, created in Christ Jesus for good works, which God prepared beforehand so that we would walk in them.*

GROW UP
Moving Past Spiritual Adolescence
EPHESIANS

Week Three: **The Walking Dead**

11 Therefore remember that formerly you, the Gentiles in the flesh, who are called "Uncircumcision" by the so-called "Circumcision," which is *performed in the flesh by human hands*—

12 remember *that you were at that time separate from Christ, excluded from the commonwealth of Israel, and strangers to the covenants of promise, having no hope and without God in the world.*

13 But now in Christ Jesus you who formerly were far off have been brought near by the blood of Christ.

14 For He Himself is our peace, who made *both* groups into *one* and broke down the barrier of the dividing wall,

15 by abolishing in His flesh the enmity, which is *the Law of commandments* contained *in ordinances, so that in Himself He might make the two into one new man*, thus *establishing peace,*

16 and might reconcile them both in one body to God through the cross, by it having put to death the enmity.

17 AND HE CAME AND PREACHED PEACE TO YOU WHO WERE FAR AWAY, AND PEACE TO THOSE WHO WERE NEAR;

18 for through Him we both have our access in one Spirit to the Father.

19 So then you are no longer strangers and aliens, but you are fellow citizens with the saints, and are of God's household,

20 having been built on the foundation of the apostles and prophets, Christ Jesus Himself being the corner stone,

21 in whom the whole building, being fitted together, is growing into a holy temple in the Lord,

22 in whom you also are being built together into a dwelling of God in the Spirit.

DISCUSS with your GROUP or PONDER on your own . . .

What key words did you notice? What seems to be Paul's main train of thought in Ephesians 2?

Look back specifically at verses 1-10. What is Paul's main point?

Digging Deeper

Sin and Death

In Ephesians 2, Paul spells out the basics of the Gospel. Mankind is dead in sin, and God makes His children alive in Christ by grace through faith. To those who have received this gift, nothing could be more clear. If you have some extra time this week, think through the Bible (using a combination of your very own brain and any search tools you have at your disposal!) to compile a summary of what God says throughout His Word about the relationship between sin and death. I'm going to give you a couple of passages you won't want to miss, but after that it's up to you to scour the Scriptures so you'll know better for yourself what God's Word says and so that you'll be better able to communicate it to others.

Genesis 3

Other Old Testament Passages

Romans 5 (especially verses 6-21)

Other New Testament Passages

Summary

LOOKING CLOSER . . .

OBSERVE the TEXT of SCRIPTURE

READ Ephesians 2:1-3 and **MARK** references to *sin*, including synonyms. Then **UNDERLINE** what the recipients "were."

Ephesians 2:1-3

1   *And you were dead in your trespasses and sins,*

2   *in which you formerly walked according to the course of this world, according to the prince of the power of the air, of the spirit that is now working in the sons of disobedience.*

3   *Among them we too all formerly lived in the lusts of our flesh, indulging the desires of the flesh and of the mind, and were by nature children of wrath, even as the rest.*

DISCUSS with your GROUP or PONDER on your own . . .

How does Paul describe the condition of his readers (and himself) before God intervened? What caused it? Were any immune? Why/why not?

How are sin and death related? Explain your answer from Scripture.

What did you learn from marking references to sin? Be sure to include what characterizes a life lived in it.

ONE STEP FURTHER:

Word Studies: Trespasses, Sins, and Transgressions

In the course of the first five verses of Ephesians 2, Paul uses several different words for "sin." If you have time, see if you can find the Greek words that are translated "trespasses," "sins," and "transgressions." Then observe how they're used elsewhere in the New Testament and see what you can discover about each. If you see other synonyms for sin, you might want to check those out, too. Then, record below what you learn.

Trespasses

Sins

Transgressions

GROW UP

Moving Past Spiritual Adolescence
EPHESIANS

When people sin, who are they walking in step with? What problems will this cause?

What do the flesh and the mind have to do with sin?

Do you think most people today have an understanding of sin? Do you think it is important? Why/why not?

ONE STEP FURTHER:

Children of Wrath

What are "children of wrath"? Spend some time unpacking this phrase this week. Start by investigating how the words "children" and "wrath" are used separately in the New Testament. Then consider the context closely as you think through what the phrase could mean and what it likely means. When you've done your own study, consult a commentary or two to see what they have to say. Then record your findings below.

OBSERVE the TEXT of SCRIPTURE

READ Ephesians 2:4-7 and **MARK** every reference to *God* and *Christ*, including pronouns.

Ephesians 2:4-7

4 *But God, being rich in mercy, because of His great love with which He loved us,*

5 *even when we were dead in our transgressions, made us alive together with Christ (by grace you have been saved),*

6 *and raised us up with Him, and seated us with Him in the heavenly* places *in Christ Jesus,*

7 *so that in the ages to come He might show the surpassing riches of His grace in kindness toward us in Christ Jesus.*

DISCUSS with your GROUP or PONDER on your own . . .

What did God do for us? Why was He rich in mercy toward us?

GROW UP

Moving Past Spiritual Adolescence
EPHESIANS

FYI:

Romans 8 and the Hope of What Is to Come . . .

14 For all who are being led by the Spirit of God, these are sons of God.

15 For you have not received a spirit of slavery leading to fear again, but you have received a spirit of adoption as sons by which we cry out, "Abba! Father!"

16 The Spirit Himself testifies with our spirit that we are children of God,

17 and if children, heirs also, heirs of God and fellow heirs with Christ, if indeed we suffer with Him so that we may also be glorified with Him.

18 For I consider that the sufferings of this present time are not worthy to be compared with the glory that is to be revealed to us.

19 For the anxious longing of the creation waits eagerly for the revealing of the sons of God.

20 For the creation was subjected to futility, not willingly, but because of Him who subjected it, in hope

21 that the creation itself also will be set free from its slavery to corruption into the freedom of the glory of the children of God.

22 For we know that the whole creation groans and suffers the pains of childbirth together until now.

23 And not only this, but also we ourselves, having the first fruits of the Spirit, even we ourselves groan within ourselves, waiting eagerly for our adoption as sons, the redemption of our body.

24 For in hope we have been saved, but hope that is seen is not hope; for who hopes for what he already sees?

25 But if we hope for what we do not see, with perseverance we wait eagerly for it.

—Romans 8:14-25

Week Three: **The Walking Dead**

What else did you learn about God from these verses?

What general condition were we in when God loved us? What was that like specifically in *your* life?

How should this impact the way we treat others who are currently dead in their sins? How are you doing at this? How could you improve?

What effect do God's actions toward us have on us both now and in the future? Explain.

What does this all have to do with Christ Jesus?

GROW UP
Moving Past Spiritual Adolescence
EPHESIANS

Digging Deeper

Faith, Works, and Fruit

While there is nothing man can do to save himself, the Bible clearly teaches that God's children bear the image of Christ (Romans 8:29; Colossians 3:10) and thus have a "family resemblance." If you have time this week, invest in studying the relationships between faith, works, and fruit. I'm going to give you some general guidelines for starting, but most of the questions you'll ask will be your own! Have fun and get digging!

• Find Greek and Hebrew words that relate to our topic. You'll also want to investigate the word "righteousness" as you'll find that it is relevant to the topic as well.

• Identify what the Bible says about how righteousness was reckoned to people in the Old Testament.

• Investigate what Jesus says about fruit.

Summary:

GROW UP
Moving Past Spiritual Adolescence
EPHESIANS

Week Three: **The Walking Dead**

OBSERVE the TEXT of SCRIPTURE

READ Ephesians 2:8-10 and **MARK** every reference to *works.* Then go back and **MARK** every negative word you see (*not, no,* etc.).

Ephesians 2:8-10

8 *For by grace you have been saved through faith; and that not of yourselves, it is the gift of God;*

9 *not as a result of works, so that no one may boast.*

10 *For we are His workmanship, created in Christ Jesus for good works, which God prepared beforehand so that we would walk in them.*

FYI:

Using Commentaries
Commentaries are helpful tools after you've done your own study. You'll want to compare your findings with at least two or three authors to get balanced input.

DISCUSS with your GROUP or PONDER on your own . . .

What does Paul say has happened to his readers? How does this relate to what he talked about in verses 1-7?

What negative words does Paul use? What do these tell us about how people are *not* saved?

How does this compare with what most people think gains God's favor?

If man could work his way to God, what attitudes do you think would spring up in humans? What attitudes would spring up in *you*?

How would you describe the role of works in the life of a believer based on this passage?

How are you doing at walking in the good works God prepared beforehand for *you* to walk in?

@THE END OF THE DAY . . .

Even if we know down deep that we can't "pay the whole bill" for our salvation, we often want to at least have the satisfaction of "kicking in the tip." But God will have none of that! Yes, God created us in Christ Jesus to walk in good works, but they are the *result* of salvation, not the reason for it.

Before you call it a day, summarize Ephesians 2:1-10.

Ephesians 2:1-10

Hashtag #:

One-Sentence Summary:

My Application(s):

GROW UP
Moving Past Spiritual Adolescence
EPHESIANS

Week Three: **The Walking Dead**

WEEK FOUR
Then and Now, Far and Near

"But now in Christ Jesus you who formerly were far off have been brought near by the blood of Christ."
–Ephesians 2:13

We've already seen that apart from Jesus, sinful people "live" as the walking dead. Because *all* have sinned (you and me included!) we know what that's like. We know the pain of being separated from God and often we'd rather forget it entirely.

Paul, though, prompts his Gentile readers to remember their former condition of alienation and separation as they embrace the peace that comes with being part of the household of God, having been reconciled and brought near by the blood of Christ.

REMEMBERING

Take a few minutes to summarize Ephesians 1. Outline it, comment on it, whatever you need to do to help you remember and apply it.

What truth have you been most actively applying?

WEEKLY READ-THROUGH #1

Version I read:

New observations/questions:

WEEKLY READ-THROUGH #2

Version I read:

New observations/questions:

WEEKLY READ-THROUGH #3

Version I read:

New observations/questions:

EPHESIANS 2

Briefly summarize Ephesians 2:1-10

OBSERVE the TEXT of SCRIPTURE

READ Ephesians 2:11-18. **MARK** every reference to Paul's Gentile readers and **UNDERLINE** every phrase that describes them. Then **MARK** every occurrence of *peace.*

Ephesians 2:11-18

11 Therefore remember that formerly you, the Gentiles in the flesh, who are called "Uncircumcision" by the so-called "Circumcision," which is performed in the flesh by human hands—

12 remember that you were at that time separate from Christ, excluded from the commonwealth of Israel, and strangers to the covenants of promise, having no hope and without God in the world.

13 But now in Christ Jesus you who formerly were far off have been brought near by the blood of Christ.

14 For He Himself is our peace, who made both groups into one and broke down the barrier of the dividing wall,

15 by abolishing in His flesh the enmity, which is the Law of commandments contained in ordinances, so that in Himself He might make the two into one new man, thus establishing peace,

16 and might reconcile them both in one body to God through the cross, by it having put to death the enmity.

17 AND HE CAME AND PREACHED PEACE TO YOU WHO WERE FAR AWAY, AND PEACE TO THOSE WHO WERE NEAR;

18 for through Him we both have our access in one Spirit to the Father.

GROW UP

Moving Past Spiritual Adolescence
EPHESIANS

Notes

DISCUSS with your GROUP or PONDER on your own . . .

What significant word starts this section of the text? What does it refer back to? How does it tie into what follows it?

How does Paul address the people he's writing to? What other words does he use to describe them and their condition?

Who does he compare them with? If the Gentiles were the "out" group, who was the "in" group? Explain.

What does Paul command them to do in verse 11?

What impact does remembering what God has saved you from have on you?

How did the "far out" Gentiles get "near" according to verse 13?

What did you learn about the person and work of Christ Jesus in verses 13-22? Make a list and be sure to include the verse references.

What did you learn by marking peace? Again, make a list.

What "undoing" was involved in establishing peace? What obstacles had to be removed?

In establishing peace, what did Christ make the two groups into? What common benefits do they share?

How does peace with God impact the way we live before Him? Since Jesus is your peace if you are in relationship with Him, how are you doing at being a peacemaker with others both in the Church and outside of it?

ONE STEP FURTHER:

Word Study: Peace

Take some time this week to identify the Greek word Paul uses that is translated "peace." Then see how he uses it first in Ephesians and then in his other letters. When you're done with that, see how it is used elsewhere in the New Testament. Record below what you learn.

GROW UP
Moving Past Spiritual Adolescence
EPHESIANS

How are you doing at showing others how *they* can have peace with God?

Peace with God
Therefore, having been justified by faith, we have peace with God through our Lord Jesus Christ, through whom also we have obtained our introduction by faith into this grace in which we stand; and we exult in hope of the glory of God.

—Romans 5:1-2

How does Paul define "the enmity" in verse 15? (Answer from the text only.)

To help shine some light on this verse, read Colossians 2:13-19. How did Christ put to death the enmity of the Law of commandments?

Remembering what we've already seen in Ephesians 1, what powers all righteous and reconciled living?

The Peace of Christ
Let the peace of Christ rule in your hearts, to which indeed you were called in one body; and be thankful.

—Colossians 3:15

What two groups did Jesus reconcile to God at the cross? What does this tell you about how all people are saved?

How can you share this truth with those who think "All roads lead to heaven"?

GROW UP
Moving Past Spiritual Adolescence
EPHESIANS

Digging Deeper

Reconciliation

We see reconciliation at its finest at the cross! This week, take some time to read a few cross-references on reconciliation and then begin to think through how we can live reconciled to one another.

Colossians 1:20-22

Romans 5:10

2 Corinthians 5:18-20

How does God reconciling us to Himself differ from men reconciling with one another?

What do you think is needed for human reconciliation to happen?

Why do you think it is often so difficult?

What other biblical passages do you think shed light on this topic?

What can you do to be part of the solution?

GROW UP
Moving Past Spiritual Adolescence
EPHESIANS

OBSERVE the TEXT of SCRIPTURE

READ Ephesians 2:19-22 and again **MARK** every reference to Paul's Gentile readers and **UNDERLINE** every phrase that describes them.

Ephesians 2:19-22

19 *So then you are no longer strangers and aliens, but you are fellow citizens with the saints, and are of God's household,*

20 *having been built on the foundation of the apostles and prophets, Christ Jesus Himself being the corner stone,*

21 *in whom the whole building, being fitted together, is growing into a holy temple in the Lord,*

22 *in whom you also are being built together into a dwelling of God in the Spirit.*

DISCUSS with your GROUP or PONDER on your own . . .

What specifically has changed for Gentile believers? How does Paul describe them? What are they now part of?

What is the foundation?

Based on this passage, what would you say to someone who thinks that the Church has replaced Israel as God's people? Explain your thinking clearly from this text and any others you want to use.

Where did the presence of God dwell in the Old Testament? (See Exodus 40:34-38; 1 Kings 8:1-11.)

ONE STEP FURTHER:

Household of God

If you have some extra time this week, see what the author of Hebrews and the apostle Peter have to say about the household of God.

Hebrews 3:1-6

1 Peter 2:5

How does this compare with the building Paul is writing about?

Who is making this building? Who else is a part of the process?

What implications does this have for you in your relationship to others? How are you doing with that?

Looking back at all of Ephesians 2, compile a chart comparing the former reality with the current one for Gentile believers.

What Was	What Is

Notes

ONE STEP FURTHER:

Word Studies:
Paul packs a load of house and temple terminology in the latter part of Ephesians 2. Here are a few words you may want to explore this week:

aliens (v. 19)

household (v. 19)

building (v. 21)

temple (v. 21)

being built together (v. 22)

dwelling (v. 22)

GROW UP
Moving Past Spiritual Adolescence
EPHESIANS

Week Four: **Then and Now, Far and Near**

Digging Deeper

Grafting In

If you have some extra time this week, read through Romans 11 to see how Paul pictures believing Gentiles in relationship to the Jewish people.

According to Romans 11:1-5, what is the relationship between God and Israel when Paul is writing? What is the basis of the relationship?

What emotional effect will Gentile salvation have on the Jewish people? What long-term outcome will this lead to for them? For the Gentiles?

What picture does Paul use to describe how Gentiles believers are related to Jewish believers?

According to Romans 11:25, how does Paul describe what is happening in Israel now? How does this compare with how God worked with Israel during Old Testament times?

How does God's work among Gentiles now compare with how He worked in Old Testament times? If you can, give some specific examples of Gentiles who had a relationship with God in the Old Testament.

How do both Jewish people and Gentiles come to God?

GROW UP
Moving Past Spiritual Adolescence
EPHESIANS

@THE END OF THE DAY . . .

Before you call it a day, take some time to think through what you've studied in the letter to the Ephesians so far. Trace in your mind Paul's train of thought so you have enough of the outline in your head to easily explain it to someone else. Once you have that, jot it down below. Finally, come up with a hashtag and one-sentence summary for Ephesians 2:11-22 . . . and live out what you're learning!

Ephesians 1

Ephesians 2:1-10

Ephesians 2:11-22

Hashtag #:

One-Sentence Summary:

My Application(s):

Week Four: **Then and Now, Far and Near**

WEEK FIVE
God's Mystery Revealed!

"... the mystery of Christ ... to be specific, that the Gentiles are fellow heirs and fellow members of the body, and fellow partakers of the promise in Christ Jesus through the gospel ..."
–Ephesians 3:4b, 6

It took a message from Jesus Himself to convince Paul of the reality of Jesus as Messiah and for him to understand God's mystery in Christ. Paul had followed hard after God in his Judaism. He knew that God had counted Abraham's faith as righteousness and he knew that God had grafted in Gentiles along the way—like Rahab and Ruth—when they became proselytes. The idea, though, that God's endgame had always been Jews and Gentiles as one body in Christ was a plot twist no one, especially not a Hebrew of Hebrews like Paul, could ever have expected!

Week Five: **God's Mystery Revealed!**

REMEMBERING

Take a few minutes to summarize the main points of Ephesians 1 and 2.

What truth is striking deepest in your life right now? Why and how?

WEEKLY READ-THROUGH #1

Version I read:

New observations/questions:

FYI:

Are you remembering to pray?

Jesus tells us in John 16:13 that when the Spirit of truth comes, He will guide us into all the truth. It's important for us to remember to pray that the Holy Spirit will be our Teacher and Guide as we study the Word.

WEEKLY READ-THROUGH #2

Version I read:

New observations/questions:

WEEKLY READ-THROUGH #3

Version I read:

New observations/questions:

EPHESIANS 3

While Ephesians 1 unfolds the beauty and riches of being in Christ, Ephesians 2 reminds us what life was like as the walking dead. In Ephesians 3, God reveals the mystery that has been hidden for ages!

OBSERVE the TEXT of SCRIPTURE

READ Ephesians 3 and **MARK** key, repeated words in a distinctive fashion. In this section, in particular, watch for contrasting pairs of words and concepts.

Ephesians 3

1 *For this reason I, Paul, the prisoner of Christ Jesus for the sake of you Gentiles—*

2 *if indeed you have heard of the stewardship of God's grace which was given to me for you;*

3 *that by revelation there was made known to me the mystery, as I wrote before in brief.*

4 *By referring to this, when you read you can understand my insight into the mystery of Christ,*

5 *which in other generations was not made known to the sons of men, as it has now been revealed to His holy apostles and prophets in the Spirit;*

6 *to be specific, that the Gentiles are fellow heirs and fellow members of the body, and fellow partakers of the promise in Christ Jesus through the gospel,*

7 *of which I was made a minister, according to the gift of God's grace which was given to me according to the working of His power.*

8 *To me, the very least of all saints, this grace was given, to preach to the Gentiles the unfathomable riches of Christ,*

9 *and to bring to light what is the administration of the mystery which for ages has been hidden in God who created all things;*

10 *so that the manifold wisdom of God might now be made known through the church to the rulers and the authorities in the heavenly places.*

GROW UP
Moving Past Spiritual Adolescence
EPHESIANS

Week Five: **God's Mystery Revealed!**

11 This was *in accordance with the eternal purpose which He carried out in Christ Jesus our Lord,*

12 *in whom we have boldness and confident access through faith in Him.*

13 *Therefore I ask you not to lose heart at my tribulations on your behalf, for they are your glory.*

14 *For this reason I bow my knees before the Father,*

15 *from whom every family in heaven and on earth derives its name,*

16 *that He would grant you, according to the riches of His glory, to be strengthened with power through His Spirit in the inner man,*

17 *so that Christ may dwell in your hearts through faith;* and *that you, being rooted and grounded in love,*

18 *may be able to comprehend with all the saints what is the breadth and length and height and depth,*

19 *and to know the love of Christ which surpasses knowledge, that you may be filled up to all the fullness of God.*

20 *Now to Him who is able to do far more abundantly beyond all that we ask or think, according to the power that works within us,*

21 *to Him be the glory in the church and in Christ Jesus to all generations forever and ever. Amen.*

DISCUSS with your GROUP or PONDER on your own . . .

What did you initially observe from the text?

What key words and/or phrases did you notice?

Briefly summarize Ephesians 3.

LOOKING EVEN CLOSER . . .

After having taken a short side road in Ephesians 2:11-21, Paul takes more time on "the mystery" before returning to his main train of thought. Let's take a look!

OBSERVE the TEXT of SCRIPTURE

READ Ephesians 3:1-7 and **MARK** every reference to *mystery*. Also **MARK** every reference to the *Gentiles*.

Ephesians 3:1-7

1 For this reason I, Paul, the prisoner of Christ Jesus for the sake of you Gentiles—

2 if indeed you have heard of the stewardship of God's grace which was given to me for you;

3 that by revelation there was made known to me the mystery, as I wrote before in brief.

4 By referring to this, when you read you can understand my insight into the mystery of Christ,

5 which in other generations was not made known to the sons of men, as it has now been revealed to His holy apostles and prophets in the Spirit;

6 to be specific, *that the Gentiles are fellow heirs and fellow members of the body, and fellow partakers of the promise in Christ Jesus through the gospel,*

7 of which I was made a minister, according to the gift of God's grace which was given to me according to the working of His power.

DISCUSS with your GROUP or PONDER on your own . . .

How does Paul describe himself in this section? Who is Paul "working for"? Explain your answer.

What does Paul have to do with God's plan for the Gentiles? What had been given to him and for what purpose? (See also Galatians 1:11-24.)

ONE STEP FURTHER:

A Prisoner for the Gentiles
If you have some time this week, look further into the circumstances surrounding Paul's imprisonment to see what you can learn about how this situation was "for the sake of" the Gentiles. Record what you discover below.

FYI:

For this reason . . .
Paul starts off Ephesians 3:1 heading toward a prayer for the Gentiles ("For this reason I, Paul, the prisoner of Christ Jesus . . .") but interrupts himself to talk more about the mystery of Christ. He picks up with his prayer again in Ephesians 3:14 with similar language ("For this reason I bow my knees before the Father . . .").

GROW UP
Moving Past Spiritual Adolescence
EPHESIANS

Week Five: **God's Mystery Revealed!**

Where does Paul's knowledge of God's mystery come from? What kind of authority does that give him?

ONE STEP FURTHER:

Word Study: *oikonomia*
If you have the time, explore Paul's use of the Greek word *oikonomia*. It's translated "administration" in Ephesians 1:10 and 3:9 but "stewardship" in Ephesians 3:2. See how Paul uses it in the New Testament. Then, record your findings below.

Who else had the mystery been revealed to and how?

What did you learn by marking *mystery* in the text? (Make a list!) What specifically is the mystery according to verse 6?

What changed with regard to the mystery during Paul's time?

Looking back at your markings as a guide, list everything this section of the text says about the Gentiles.

What benefits does Paul say the Gentiles now have? How did this change their status with Jewish believers? What ramifications did the changes have on both parties?

Have you ever been in a situation where a new person or group encroached on something that was "yours"? Perhaps it was the birth of a sibling, the addition of a person to the family through marriage. What kind of challenges did you face?

What challenges do we face in the church today being "fellows" (heirs, members, and partakers) with others who are different from us?

How are you doing at being a "fellow" in the body?

How did Paul become a minister of the gospel? What powered his ministry? What powers yours?

ONE STEP FURTHER:

Word Study: Grace
If you have the time, find the Greek word translated "grace" and trace Paul's use of it in Ephesians and throughout the rest of his letters. Then see how it's translated in the remainder of the New Testament. Record what you learn below.

GROW UP
Moving Past Spiritual Adolescence
EPHESIANS

Week Five: **God's Mystery Revealed!**

Digging Deeper

Revelation in the Life of Paul

If you have time this week, see what you can discover about revelation in Paul's life. Start with his conversion on the road to Damascus—I'll give you the reference for that! Then, using your own study skills, find other truths God revealed to Paul directly and how Paul directs his readers to find truth.

Paul's Conversion—Acts 9:1-31:

Revelation in Paul's Life (Not sure where to start? Think through good search terms for blueletterbible.com and go from there.)

What revelation does Paul point believers to? (Don't miss 2 Timothy 3:16-17 in your study!)

LOOKING EVEN CLOSER . . .
OBSERVE the TEXT of SCRIPTURE

READ Ephesians 3:8-13 and **MARK** every reference to *God*. Also **MARK** every reference to the *Gentiles*.

Ephesians 3:8-13

8 *To me, the very least of all saints, this grace was given, to preach to the Gentiles the unfathomable riches of Christ,*

9 *and to bring to light what is the administration of the mystery which for ages has been hidden in God who created all things;*

10 *so that the manifold wisdom of God might now be made known through the church to the rulers and the authorities in the heavenly places.*

11 *This was in accordance with the eternal purpose which He carried out in Christ Jesus our Lord,*

12 *in whom we have boldness and confident access through faith in Him.*

13 *Therefore I ask you not to lose heart at my tribulations on your behalf, for they are your glory.*

> **FYI:**
>
> **Saints!**
> When Paul uses the word "saints" (Greek: *hagios*) he is simply referring to believers, those who are set apart and made holy for God. If you belong to Jesus, you're a saint too!

DISCUSS with your GROUP or PONDER on your own . . .

How does Paul describe himself in verse 8? Does it surprise you? How does his view of himself compare with your view of yourself?

Why was Paul able to minister and preach as he did?

What message did God give him to deliver to the Gentiles?

GROW UP
Moving Past Spiritual Adolescence
EPHESIANS

Week Five: **God's Mystery Revealed!**

What was Paul bringing to light?

Who kept the mystery a secret and why?

What does the Church have to do with the revelation of the mystery?

What do we know about God's "eternal purpose" both from Ephesians and elsewhere? Who does it involve? Who does it hinge on? (Check out Romans 8:28-29, Romans 9:11, Ephesians 1:11, and 2 Timothy 1:9.)

Compare this with Ephesians 1:4-5. From before the foundation of the world, who had God chosen? In whom? How are they related to one another?

Think for a moment about the implications of God revealing His eternal purpose in Christ through the Church. What does this tell us about the fall? About man's rebellion? Did anything catch God off guard? What difference does this make?

According to this passage, what benefits do believers (both Jew and Gentile) have in Christ?

If you're a Gentile believer, what difference does the fact that you're not part of a "Plan B" make to you?

What emotional state does Paul warn against in verse 13? Is this something you ever deal with? Under what circumstance(s)?

Finally, what further truths did you learn about God from this section of Ephesians? Take some time to prayerfully reflect and respond.

Week Five: **God's Mystery Revealed!**

LET'S LOOK CLOSER . . .

In Ephesians 3:1-13, Paul unpacked and defined "the mystery of Christ" as the truth that the Gentiles are fellow heirs, members of the body, and partakers of the promise in Christ Jesus through the Gospel. Jesus was not a Savior for the Jews only; He was and is the Savior of the whole world! As we move into the rest of the chapter, we'll see Paul's prayer for the Ephesians in response to this overwhelming theological truth!

Before we forge ahead, think for a moment about your prayer life. When you pray, what do you pray for? Aunt Mary's bunions? More money at work? The salvation of your neighbors? We pray for a myriad of things and Scripture teaches us to bring our cares and concerns to our God—everything from the bunions to the bills. Peter is clear about this in 1 Peter 5:7 when he says we are to cast all our cares on God because He cares for us. Still, it's instructive for us to look at Paul's heart as he prays for the Ephesian believers! Let's go phrase by phrase to see what he prays and what results he expects God to give!

OBSERVE the TEXT of SCRIPTURE

READ Ephesians 3:14-21 and **MARK** in a distinct way every reference to *God the Father*, every reference to *Christ*, and every reference to the *Spirit*. Be careful to **MARK** the appropriate pronouns also.

Ephesians 3:14-21

14   *For this reason I bow my knees before the Father,*

15   *from whom every family in heaven and on earth derives its name,*

16   *that He would grant you, according to the riches of His glory, to be strengthened with power through His Spirit in the inner man,*

17   *so that Christ may dwell in your hearts through faith; and that you, being rooted and grounded in love,*

18   *may be able to comprehend with all the saints what is the breadth and length and height and depth,*

19   *and to know the love of Christ which surpasses knowledge, that you may be filled up to all the fullness of God.*

20   *Now to Him who is able to do far more abundantly beyond all that we ask or think, according to the power that works within us,*

21   *to Him be the glory in the church and in Christ Jesus to all generations forever and ever. Amen.*

DISCUSS with your GROUP or PONDER on your own . . .

Looking back at where you marked references to God the Father, list what you learned about Him from the text.

Now, do the same for Christ.

Finally, list what you learned about the Spirit.

LOOKING EVEN CLOSER . . . and MEMORIZING!!!

Please don't shut your workbook and run! I realize you may never have memorized Scripture before or it may be *years* since you have. Would you give it a try this week? Memorizing is the seldom talked about powerhouse observation tool! As we start examining Paul's prayer, our first step in memorizing will be to simply note and remember the **God–Gentiles–God** pattern. You'll see what I mean as we get started if you watch the section headings.

OBSERVE the TEXT of SCRIPTURE

READ Ephesians 3:14-15 and again **MARK** every reference to *Paul* including pronouns.

Ephesians 3:14-15 — God: The One Paul Prays To

14 For this reason I bow my knees before the Father,

15 from whom every family in heaven and on earth derives its name,

DISCUSS with your GROUP or PONDER on your own . . .

What is Paul doing? What posture does he take? Do you think this is important? Why/why not?

ONE STEP FURTHER:

Paul Prayed to the Father

In Ephesians 3 it's clear that Paul directed his prayer to the Father. It's not uncommon at all today to hear prayers directed to other members of the Trinity. Have you ever wondered if that's biblical? This week, take some time to search the Scriptures to see what roles the Father, the Son, and the Spirit play in prayer. Then record what you discover below.

GROW UP
Moving Past Spiritual Adolescence
EPHESIANS

Week Five: **God's Mystery Revealed!**

How does Paul refer to God and describe Him in verse 14? Why is this important?

Taking vv. 15 and 16 together, in what sense do you think he is using the term "Father"?

Looking back in the text, where does Paul pick this prayer up from? What does it connect back to? (Look back for an incomplete sentence . . .)

Why is he praying?

INDUCTIVE FOCUS:

Scripture Doesn't Contradict Scripture

When we're faced with portions of Scripture that say different things, we need to remember the interpretive principle that Scripture never contradicts Scripture. Furthermore, we should interpret unclear passages in light of clear passages. These principles will help you this week as you consider what Paul meant when he said that "every family in heaven and on earth derives its name" from the Father.

As you examine what this means, you need to consider whether "every family" (3:15) includes everyone or just believers. See what you can find that would support each position.

Digging Deeper

Let's Start to Memorize . . .

As we go through the text, I'm going to use **bold face** for the **verses** we're memorizing and include *prompt questions* in *italics* to help you think through what you're learning. I'd highly suggest that you write out the memory portion and at least think through the prompts to help you remember the flow of thought.

For this reason (*What reason?*) [Memorize 3 words]

(*What does he do?* He prays.)   (*Where?* and *To Whom?*)
I bow my knees   **before the Father** [Memorize 7 words]

(*What do we know about the Father?*)
from whom every family in heaven and on earth derives its name... [12 words]

OBSERVE the TEXT of SCRIPTURE

READ Ephesians 3:16-19 and **MARK** every reference to the Gentiles (you'll be looking mainly for *you* and *your*). Then **UNDERLINE** everything Paul prays for them. As we read, let's watch for references to the Trinity, remembering that Paul prays *to* the Father.

Ephesians 3:16-19 — Gentiles: The Ones Paul Prays For . . .

16 *that He would grant you, according to the riches of His glory, to be strengthened with power through His Spirit in the inner man,*

17 *so that Christ may dwell in your hearts through faith; and that you, being rooted and grounded in love,*

18 *may be able to comprehend with all the saints what is the breadth and length and height and depth,*

19 *and to know the love of Christ which surpasses knowledge, that you may be filled up to all the fullness of God.*

DISCUSS with your GROUP or PONDER on your own . . .

According to verse 16, what does Paul pray that the Father would grant the Ephesians? How?

Who brings this about in your inner man and with what resources?

Take a moment to review Ephesians 1:19-21. What did/does the power of God do according to these verses?

Are you living today strengthened with power through His Spirit in the inner man? If so, how?

ONE STEP FURTHER:

Word Studies: Strengthened and Power

Take some time this week to investigate the Greek words translated "strengthened" and "power." See where and how Paul uses them in Ephesians and in the rest of his letters. Then see how they're used in the rest of the New Testament. Record below what you discover and how it helps you understand "strengthened with power through His Spirit" better.

GROW UP
Moving Past Spiritual Adolescence
EPHESIANS

Week Five: **God's Mystery Revealed!**

Would you like someone to pray Ephesians 3:16 on your behalf? Who can you pray it for? How can living in light of this reality change the way you think and respond to life's trials?

What does Paul pray for the Ephesians' hearts in verse 17? What does this have to do with love?

How is your life demonstrating that it is rooted and grounded in love? What does it have to do with faith?

To the best of your ability, describe how the Father, the Son, and the Spirit work together according to this passage.

According to verses 18, what result does Paul expect?

Let's compare verse 18 with what Paul has already said in Ephesians 2:13. What do saints who were formerly sinners know? Is there anyone who is too far away to be saved?

How does "knowing" the love of Christ compare to "knowledge"? How do you resolve this apparent contradiction?

Who in your life needs to know these truths?

According to verse 19, what other result does Paul expect for the Ephesians?

Let's take a look at this word "fullness" in other places in Ephesians. We'll also look at its occurrences in Colossians since the letters are closely related and have much content overlap. Finally, we'll take a look at a verse from John that refers to Jesus.

Ephesians 1:10, Ephesians 1:22-23, Ephesians 4:13

Colossians 1:19, Colossians 2:9

John 1:16

Now, having looked at these cross-references for help, how would you explain what Paul means when he says being "filled up to all the fullness of God"? What roles do the Father, Son, and Spirit play in this?

Digging Deeper

Let's Memorize a Little More . . .

Remember to write out **the text** to help you remember what Paul prays for the Ephesians!

. . . that He would grant you [Memorize 5 words]

(*How will God give?*)
according to the riches of His glory [Memorize 7 words]

(*What is Paul asking for them?*)
to be strengthened with power [Memorize 5 words]

(*How?*)   (*Where?*)
through His Spirit   in the inner man, [Memorize 7 words]

(*Why/what else?*)   (*Where?*)   (*How?*)
so that Christ may dwell   in your hearts   through faith [Memorize 10 words]

(*What will that condition include?*)
and **that you, being rooted and grounded in love,** [Memorize 9 words]

(*What result does Paul expect?*)   (*With who else?*)
[you] may be able to comprehend   with all the saints [Memorize 9 words]

(*Comprehend what?*)
what is the breadth and length and height and depth,

and

to know the love of Christ which surpasses knowledge, [Memorize 20 words]

(*Why? What other result does Paul expect?*)
that you may be filled up to all the fullness of God. [Memorize 12 words]

One great way to practice this is to have someone ask you the prompt questions. You can answer with what you've memorized. Soon you'll have it treasured in your heart!

OBSERVE the TEXT of SCRIPTURE

READ Ephesians 3:20-21 and **MARK** every reference to the *God*. Then **UNDERLINE** what He is able to do.

Ephesians 3:20-21 — God: The One Paul Prays To . . .

20 *Now to Him who is able to do far more abundantly beyond all that we ask or think, according to the power that works within us,*

21 *to Him be the glory in the church and in Christ Jesus to all generations forever and ever. Amen.*

DISCUSS with your GROUP or PONDER on your own . . .

Based on verse 20, how would you describe Paul's view of God and prayer? How does this compare with yours?

Where does Paul say this power is at work?

Have you seen this verse and others like it misinterpreted and misapplied in favor of "prosperity theology"? If so, how? What in the text blocks this misinterpretation?

On the other hand, do you think people wrongly "limit" God in their asking and thinking? Do you? If so, write out a few examples.

FYI:

Treasured!
Your word I have treasured in my heart,
That I may not sin against You.
            —Psalm 119:11

GROW UP
Moving Past Spiritual Adolescence
EPHESIANS

Week Five: **God's Mystery Revealed!**

How can you think and live more biblically according to what God has given you in Christ?

FYI:

God's Wisdom and Knowledge

Oh, the depth of the riches both of the wisdom and knowledge of God! How unsearchable are His judgments and unfathomable His ways!

—Romans 11:33

@THE END OF THE DAY . . .

This has been a long week of study as Ephesians 3 is so packed with truth! Before you put your book down, take a few minutes to review and ask God to help you see what is the most important truth for you to remember and apply today. Jot it down below and ask God to keep it front and center in your mind as you go about your day.

Ephesians 3

Hashtag #:

One-Sentence Summary:

My Application(s):

WEEK SIX
Complete Unity in God-Given Diversity

"one Lord, one faith, one baptism, . . . "
–Ephesians 4:5

Try as it will over and over again, human culture cannot bring true reconciliation. Band-Aid™ fixes? Sure! Short-term gains? Absolutely! Play-nice solutions? From time to time. Why? Because true reconciliation requires more than a topical treatment; in fact, it requires more than heart surgery. True reconciliation only comes with new hearts–transplants. You can't vote it in, you can't legislate it out. Only a relationship with the Father through Jesus Christ and the power of the indwelling Spirit can bring about true unity in the midst of God-given diversity. Let's take a look!

Notes

REMEMBERING

Take a few minutes to summarize the main points from Ephesians 1 and 2.

Briefly summarize Ephesians 3.

WEEKLY READ-THROUGH #1

Version I read:

New observations/questions:

WEEKLY READ-THROUGH #2

Version I read:

New observations/questions:

GROW UP
Moving Past Spiritual Adolescence
EPHESIANS

WEEKLY READ-THROUGH #3

Version I read:

New observations/questions:

EPHESIANS 4

While content becomes a little "easier" to understand in the second half of the letter, you may find applications hitting closer to home! Remember, even when the Word of God feels like sandpaper on the rough edges of life, sanctification is a good thing and it takes a lifetime! Be encouraged!

OBSERVE the TEXT of SCRIPTURE

READ Ephesians 4 and **MARK** key words you notice.

Ephesians 4

1   Therefore I, the prisoner of the Lord, implore you to walk in a manner worthy of the calling with which you have been called,

2   with all humility and gentleness, with patience, showing tolerance for one another in love,

3   being diligent to preserve the unity of the Spirit in the bond of peace.

4   There is one body and one Spirit, just as also you were called in one hope of your calling;

5   one Lord, one faith, one baptism,

6   one God and Father of all who is over all and through all and in all.

7   But to each one of us grace was given according to the measure of Christ's gift.

GROW UP

Moving Past Spiritual Adolescence
EPHESIANS

8 Therefore it says,
"WHEN HE ASCENDED ON HIGH, HE LED CAPTIVE A HOST OF CAPTIVES,
AND HE GAVE GIFTS TO MEN."

9 (Now this expression, "He ascended," what does it mean except that He also had descended into the lower parts of the earth?

10 He who descended is Himself also He who ascended far above all the heavens, so that He might fill all things.)

11 And He gave some as apostles, and some as prophets, and some as evangelists, and some as pastors and teachers,

12 for the equipping of the saints for the work of service, to the building up of the body of Christ;

13 until we all attain to the unity of the faith, and of the knowledge of the Son of God, to a mature man, to the measure of the stature which belongs to the fullness of Christ.

14 As a result, we are no longer to be children, tossed here and there by waves and carried about by every wind of doctrine, by the trickery of men, by craftiness in deceitful scheming;

15 but speaking the truth in love, we are to grow up in all aspects into Him who is the head, even Christ,

16 from whom the whole body, being fitted and held together by what every joint supplies, according to the proper working of each individual part, causes the growth of the body for the building up of itself in love.

17 So this I say, and affirm together with the Lord, that you walk no longer just as the Gentiles also walk, in the futility of their mind,

18 being darkened in their understanding, excluded from the life of God because of the ignorance that is in them, because of the hardness of their heart;

19 and they, having become callous, have given themselves over to sensuality for the practice of every kind of impurity with greediness.

20 But you did not learn Christ in this way,

21 if indeed you have heard Him and have been taught in Him, just as truth is in Jesus,

22 that, in reference to your former manner of life, you lay aside the old self, which is being corrupted in accordance with the lusts of deceit,

23 and that you be renewed in the spirit of your mind,

24 and put on the new self, which in the likeness of God has been created in righteousness and holiness of the truth.

25 Therefore, laying aside falsehood, SPEAK TRUTH EACH ONE of you WITH HIS NEIGHBOR, for we are members of one another.

26 BE ANGRY, AND yet DO NOT SIN; do not let the sun go down on your anger,

27 and do not give the devil an opportunity.

GROW UP
Moving Past Spiritual Adolescence
EPHESIANS

28 *He who steals must steal no longer; but rather he must labor, performing with his own hands what is good, so that he will have something to share with one who has need.*

29 *Let no unwholesome word proceed from your mouth, but only such a word as is good for edification according to the need of the moment, so that it will give grace to those who hear.*

30 *Do not grieve the Holy Spirit of God, by whom you were sealed for the day of redemption.*

31 *Let all bitterness and wrath and anger and clamor and slander be put away from you, along with all malice.*

32 *Be kind to one another, tender-hearted, forgiving each other, just as God in Christ also has forgiven you.*

DISCUSS with your GROUP or PONDER on your own . . .

What did you initially observe from the text?

What key words and/or phrases did you notice?

Briefly summarize Ephesians 4.

In a little more depth, summarize Ephesians 4:1-16.

GROW UP

Moving Past Spiritual Adolescence
EPHESIANS

Week Six: **Complete Unity in God-Given Diversity**

LOOKING EVEN CLOSER . . .

Paul transitions into the application-heavy portion of his letter with a "Therefore" that carries the weight of everything he's already written.

OBSERVE the TEXT of SCRIPTURE

READ Ephesians 4:1-6 and **MARK** every reference to *calling/called*. Also **MARK** every reference to *unity* (include *one*).

Ephesians 4:1-6

1 *Therefore I, the prisoner of the Lord, implore you to walk in a manner worthy of the calling with which you have been called,*

2 *with all humility and gentleness, with patience, showing tolerance for one another in love,*

3 *being diligent to preserve the unity of the Spirit in the bond of peace.*

4 There is *one body and one Spirit, just as also you were called in one hope of your calling;*

5 *one Lord, one faith, one baptism,*

6 *one God and Father of all who is over all and through all and in all.*

DISCUSS with your GROUP or PONDER on your own . . .

What is the "Therefore" there for? Why can Paul call for a response from his readers?

How does Paul again describe himself? What does this say about his walk?

Comparing Paul's use of the word "worthy" (Greek: *axios*) in Ephesians 4:1 with its use in Romans 16:2, Philippians 1:27, Colossians 1:10, and 1 Thessalonians 2:12, how would you describe walking in a worthy manner?

How are you doing with walking worthy? What can you improve?

What did you learn by marking called/calling? What is involved in the calling? What responsibility does it bring?

What various ways does Paul describe unity in the Church?

How much attention, by comparison, do you typically give to unity in the body? How can you improve and contribute more to unity?

Based on what we've already seen about "peace" in Ephesians, how are believers bonded together in peace? What does this have to do with the body of Christ?

How would you explain the "one hope . . . one Lord, one faith, one baptism" to today's pluralistic culture?

ONE STEP FURTHER:

Word Studies: Called

If you have time this week, examine Paul's use of the word "call" in Ephesians and his other letters. As you do, look for the Greek word he uses and then see if you can identify other words in this letter that are related to it. One of them (a compound Greek word) shows up in Ephesians 4:1. Record your findings below.

GROW UP
Moving Past Spiritual Adolescence
EPHESIANS

Week Six: **Complete Unity in God-Given Diversity**

Where do you see the Trinity in Ephesians 4:1-6?

Looking back at this whole section, what does Paul implore us to do in these verses and how?

In any of this, is your behavior to hinge on others' behavior toward you? Does your current mode of operation need any adjustment? If so, how?

How does this differ from our culture's view of what makes for acceptable behavior?

What from this portion of the text do you most need to apply and how do you plan to do it?

Digging Deeper

So, what exactly is tolerant behavior?

In a "politically correct" world where "tolerance" reigns and truth offends, what are Christians to do? What "tolerance" does Paul call for in Ephesians 4:2? What exactly does this biblical word (Greek: *anechomai*) mean throughout the pages of Scripture? And what does all this have to do with how we live in our world today?

How does the world define tolerance? What, if anything, in the world's definition opposes God? Explain.

What is the biblical picture of tolerance? Make sure you include the positive and negative aspects you observed.

Based on what you've studied from God's Word, how are you to live with integrity in today's culture?

OBSERVE the TEXT of SCRIPTURE

READ Ephesians 4:7-16 and **MARK** in a distinctive way the contrasting words *ascended* and *descended*. Also **MARK** every reference to *gifts* and forms of the word. Finally, **MARK** all synonyms related to growing up.

Ephesians 4:7-16

7 But to each one of us grace was given according to the measure of Christ's gift.

8 Therefore it says,
"WHEN HE ASCENDED ON HIGH, HE LED CAPTIVE A HOST OF CAPTIVES, AND HE GAVE GIFTS TO MEN."

9 (Now this expression, "He ascended," what does it mean except that He also had descended into the lower parts of the earth?

10 He who descended is Himself also He who ascended far above all the heavens, so that He might fill all things.)

11 And He gave some as apostles, and some as prophets, and some as evangelists, and some as pastors and teachers,

GROW UP
Moving Past Spiritual Adolescence
EPHESIANS

Week Six: **Complete Unity in God-Given Diversity**

12 *for the equipping of the saints for the work of service, to the building up of the body of Christ;*

13 *until we all attain to the unity of the faith, and of the knowledge of the Son of God, to a mature man, to the measure of the stature which belongs to the fullness of Christ.*

14 *As a result, we are no longer to be children, tossed here and there by waves and carried about by every wind of doctrine, by the trickery of men, by craftiness in deceitful scheming;*

15 *but speaking the truth in love, we are to grow up in all* aspects *into Him who is the head,* even *Christ,*

16 *from whom the whole body, being fitted and held together by what every joint supplies, according to the proper working of each individual part, causes the growth of the body for the building up of itself in love.*

DISCUSS with your GROUP or PONDER on your own . . .

Unity is Paul's emphasis in verses 1-6. What kind of diversity does he have in mind in verses 7-8?

What did you learn by marking references to *gifts* in this section? What was given to whom and by whom?

Based on this list, what do you think Paul is referring to when he writes about the gifts that Christ gave to men?

We'll come back to this more in a little bit, but first let's deal with verses 8-10. Who ascended and descended and to what locations? Where do you think these locations are? Why?

In order to narrow down what Paul is talking about, let's compare other uses of "ascend" (Greek: *anabaino*; John 3:13, 6:62, and 20:17) and other uses of "descend" (Greek: *katabaino*; John 3:13, 6:33-58 ["came down"/"come[s] down"] and Romans 10:7). Do these verses help us understand the text at hand? If so, how?

What was Jesus' purpose in this? Does this remind you of anything we already saw in Ephesians 1 and 3? Explain.

What did Christ do with the captives? Who do you think the captives are? Why?

According to verse 11, what did He give to the Church and for what reason?

Who, then, is to be "doing" the ministry or service? How does this compare with the way your church operates?

ONE STEP FURTHER:

Gifts to the Church

Take some time this week to explore the gifts that God gives to the Church. What are they? How do they function? Are they active today?

Apostles

Prophets

Evangelists

Pastors

Teachers

GROW UP

Moving Past Spiritual Adolescence
EPHESIANS

Week Six: **Complete Unity in God-Given Diversity**

What is the end goal in this? What should characterize the typical Christian?

What practical results will we see according to verse 14? Why is this important?

What specific threats do Christians face in this world? How aware are you of these?

According to verse 15, what is involved in helping one another grow up? How are you doing with this?

How does the working of each part of the body affect the health of the whole? Give an example.

What affect will not properly growing spiritually have on others?

In what practical ways have others helped you to grow up in your faith?

Digging Deeper

What Else Does the Word Say About Spiritual Gifts?

There are four passages in the Bible that talk specifically about spiritual gifts. If you have some time this week, check each one of them out to see what gifts God gives and for what purpose(s).

Ephesians 4

1 Peter 4

1 Corinthians 12

Romans 12

Week Six: **Complete Unity in God-Given Diversity**

@THE END OF THE DAY . . .

Take some time to think and pray through what we've studied this week. Ask God to cement specific truths to your heart and to bring them to your remembrance throughout the week. If there is a specific area in your life where you're clinging to immaturity, why don't you write it down below and leave it there. You have a great God and it's time to grow up . . . for your good and for the good of the Body!

Before you put your pencil down, build those spiritual muscles a little more by reviewing where we've come over the past several weeks.

Ephesians 1

Ephesians 2:1-10

Ephesians 2:11-22

Ephesians 3

Ephesians 4:1-16

Hashtag #:

One-Sentence Summary:

My Application(s):

WEEK SEVEN
Use the New Mind God Gave You!

"So this I say, and affirm together with the Lord, that you walk no longer just as the Gentiles also walk, in the futility of their mind . . . and that you be renewed in the spirit of your mind . . ."
–Ephesians 4:17 and 23

Most children have heard it, most parents have said it: "Use the brain God gave you!" The problem in a broken and fallen world, though, is that the fallen mind yields only futility. Gracefully, God doesn't leave His people to cope with futile minds. In Christ, He makes us new creatures. As Paul says in 2 Corinthians 5:17: "Therefore if anyone is in Christ, *he is* a new creature; the old things passed away; behold, new things have come." Christians are being transformed by the *renewing* of their minds!

Week Seven: **Use the New Mind God Gave You!**

REMEMBERING

Take a few minutes to summarize the main points of Ephesians 1–3.

Briefly summarize what you've learned so far about Ephesians 4.

WEEKLY READ-THROUGH #1

Version I read:

New observations/questions:

WEEKLY READ-THROUGH #2

Version I read:

New observations/questions:

WEEKLY READ-THROUGH #3

Version I read:

New observations/questions:

EPHESIANS 4

Kicking off the application portion of his letter in Ephesians 4:1-16, Paul has been exhorting his readers to act in accordance with who they are in Christ, to *be* what they believe. What's on the inside will be visible on the outside!

OBSERVE the TEXT of SCRIPTURE

READ Ephesians 4:17-32 and **MARK** key words you notice.

Ephesians 4:17-32

17 *So this I say, and affirm together with the Lord, that you walk no longer just as the Gentiles also walk, in the futility of their mind,*

18 *being darkened in their understanding, excluded from the life of God because of the ignorance that is in them, because of the hardness of their heart;*

19 *and they, having become callous, have given themselves over to sensuality for the practice of every kind of impurity with greediness.*

20 *But you did not learn Christ in this way,*

21 *if indeed you have heard Him and have been taught in Him, just as truth is in Jesus,*

22 *that, in reference to your former manner of life, you lay aside the old self, which is being corrupted in accordance with the lusts of deceit,*

23 *and that you be renewed in the spirit of your mind,*

24 *and put on the new self, which in the likeness of God has been created in righteousness and holiness of the truth.*

25 *Therefore, laying aside falsehood, SPEAK TRUTH EACH ONE of you WITH HIS NEIGHBOR, for we are members of one another.*

26 *BE ANGRY, AND yet DO NOT SIN; do not let the sun go down on your anger,*

27 *and do not give the devil an opportunity.*

28 *He who steals must steal no longer; but rather he must labor, performing with his own hands what is good, so that he will have something to share with one who has need.*

Week Seven: **Use the New Mind God Gave You!**

29 *Let no unwholesome word proceed from your mouth, but only such a word as is good for edification according to the need* of the moment, *so that it will give grace to those who hear.*

30 *Do not grieve the Holy Spirit of God, by whom you were sealed for the day of redemption.*

31 *Let all bitterness and wrath and anger and clamor and slander be put away from you, along with all malice.*

32 *Be kind to one another, tender-hearted, forgiving each other, just as God in Christ also has forgiven you.*

ONE STEP FURTHER:

Brevity Exercise

Before we begin unpacking Ephesians 4:17-24, see if you can summarize each of the following sections in one keyword or hashtag. The point of this is to help you think about and *remember* the most important things in each chapter.

Ephesians 1
#

Ephesians 2
#

Ephesians 3
#

Ephesians 4:1-16
#

DISCUSS with your GROUP or PONDER on your own . . .

What did you initially observe from the text?

How does this tie in with the first half of Ephesians 4?

What questions do you want answered?

FYI:

"Affirm together"

When Paul "affirm[s] [Greek: *marturomai*] together with the Lord" he is not making a mere suggestion. He claims to be testifying on behalf of the risen Christ.

OBSERVE the TEXT of SCRIPTURE

READ Ephesians 4:17-24 and **MARK** all references to the *mind* and the *heart*. (If you can find the words that contain the Greek word for *mind* or *think*, get those, too!) Also **MARK** every occurrence of *truth*.

Ephesians 4:17-24

17 *So this I say, and affirm together with the Lord, that you walk no longer just as the Gentiles also walk, in the futility of their mind,*

18 *being darkened in their understanding, excluded from the life of God because of the ignorance that is in them, because of the hardness of their heart;*

GROW UP
Moving Past Spiritual Adolescence
EPHESIANS

19 and they, having become callous, have given themselves over to sensuality for the practice of every kind of impurity with greediness.

20 But you did not learn Christ in this way,

21 if indeed you have heard Him and have been taught in Him, just as truth is in Jesus,

22 that, in reference to your former manner of life, you lay aside the old self, which is being corrupted in accordance with the lusts of deceit,

23 and that you be renewed in the spirit of your mind,

24 and put on the new self, which in the likeness of God has been created in righteousness and holiness of the truth.

DISCUSS with your GROUP or PONDER on your own . . .

What has changed for Paul's readers? How are they no longer to walk?

Describe the heart and minds of the people before Christ. What are they like? What has happened to them? What do they do? What do they feel? What *don't* they feel?

How are these attitudes and behaviors antithetical to the Christian life?

Do you think it's possible for someone "darkened in understanding" to think they are "good with God"? Why?

FYI:

Depraved Minds

And just as they did not see fit to acknowledge God any longer, God gave them over to a depraved mind, to do those things which are not proper, being filled with all unrighteousness, wickedness, greed, evil; full of envy, murder, strife, deceit, malice; they are gossips, slanderers, haters of God, insolent, arrogant, boastful, inventors of evil, disobedient to parents, without understanding, untrustworthy, unloving, unmerciful; and although they know the ordinance of God, that those who practice such things are worthy of death, they not only do the same, but also give hearty approval to those who practice them.

—Romans 1:28-32

ONE STEP FURTHER:

Culpable Ignorance

Commentators refer to the "futility of mind" that Paul talks about in Ephesians 4:17 as a "culpable ignorance." If you have some time this week, read Romans 1:18-32 to see how it helps to explain this condition. Record your observations below.

GROW UP

Moving Past Spiritual Adolescence
EPHESIANS

GROW UP
Moving Past Spiritual Adolescence
EPHESIANS

Hearts of Stone and Flesh

"Moreover, I will give you a new heart and put a new spirit within you; and I will remove the heart of stone from your flesh and give you a heart of flesh. I will put My Spirit within you and cause you to walk in My statutes, and you will be careful to observe My ordinances."

—Ezekiel 36:26-27

Week Seven: **Use the New Mind God Gave You!**

How would you respond to someone who lives in darkness but claims to know God?

In verse 20, Paul says, "But you did not learn Christ in this way." From the text, what do you think he is referring to by the phrase "in this way"?

What does the phrase "learn Christ" imply?

What are believers to lay aside? What are they to put on and do instead? Why?

What is central to the renewing of the mind? How does it contrast with the old self?

How does our culture's view of truth come into play here?

Digging Deeper

What is Truth?

The first post-modern thinker showed up in history long before "modern" came. In questioning Jesus, Pilate addressed this post-modern skepticism in John 18:38—"*What is truth?*"—to the Way, the Truth, and the Life Himself. Take some time this week to explore what the Bible says about what truth is and where it is found. I'll give you some general categories, but you take it from there!

Torah

History

Wisdom Literature

Prophets

Gospels

Acts

Epistles

Apocalyptic Literature

Culture's View of Truth:

God's View of Truth:

How I can share the Truth with my culture:

Week Seven: **Use the New Mind God Gave You!**

OBSERVE the TEXT of SCRIPTURE

READ Ephesians 4:25-32 and **MARK** key words *you* notice.

Ephesians 4:25-32

25 *Therefore, laying aside falsehood, SPEAK TRUTH EACH ONE of you WITH HIS NEIGHBOR, for we are members of one another.*

26 *BE ANGRY, AND yet DO NOT SIN; do not let the sun go down on your anger,*

27 *and do not give the devil an opportunity.*

28 *He who steals must steal no longer; but rather he must labor, performing with his own hands what is good, so that he will have something to share with one who has need.*

29 *Let no unwholesome word proceed from your mouth, but only such a word as is good for edification according to the need of the moment, so that it will give grace to those who hear.*

30 *Do not grieve the Holy Spirit of God, by whom you were sealed for the day of redemption.*

31 *Let all bitterness and wrath and anger and clamor and slander be put away from you, along with all malice.*

32 *Be kind to one another, tender-hearted, forgiving each other, just as God in Christ also has forgiven you.*

INDUCTIVE FOCUS:

Doing Your Own Word Study
Doing your own word study involves more than just looking up a word in a Bible dictionary or word study tool. Although these tools are important, the groundwork for a word study involves using a concordance to locate every occurrence of the word and its related word-group members in the text of Scripture and checking them out in context. Running to a word study book first is like running to a commentary before reading the text of Scripture—people do it, but it's full of spoilers!

DISCUSS with your GROUP or PONDER on your own . . .

How does verse 25 relate to verses 17-24?

How is speaking truth a "corporate event" according to verse 25?

How are you at speaking truth? At receiving truth?

GROW UP
Moving Past Spiritual Adolescence
EPHESIANS

Looking through verses 26-29, note the behaviors Paul tells his readers to replace and the respective benefits. I'll fill one in as an example.

Don't Do This	Instead Do This	For This Benefit
Let sun go down on anger	Resolve issues quickly	Not giving devil opportunity

How do these particular sins affect unity in the body? How do the correlating "insteads" promote and foster unity?

In verse 30, Paul says not to grieve (Greek: *lupeo*) the Holy Spirit of God. Why do you think believers are able to do this, and how do they do it?

What else does Paul say to put away? What should be present instead and why?

Let's look at a few other verses to help us understand some of the elements of:

• Kindness (Matthew 11:30 translated "easy"; Luke 6:35; Romans 2:4; 1 Peter 2:3)

• Tender-heartedness (1 Peter 3:8 translated "kindhearted")

Stuff to Dump

If you have time, see what distinguishes each of these sinful cousins:

Bitterness

Wrath

Anger

Clamor

Slander

Malice

If the Spirit nudges you about any of these, take some time to pray and consider how you can counteract these with kindness, tender-heartedness, and forgiveness. Record below what you need to remember.

Week Seven: **Use the New Mind God Gave You!**

• Forgiveness (Luke 7:42-43; Colossians 2:13; Colossians 3:13)

What are some ways you can be kind, tender-hearted, and forgiving this week?

What are some ways you can use *words* to build people up?

@THE END OF THE DAY . . .

As best you can, think through and write down how *you* can be part of unity and part of building up your local church in the way you handle truth, in the way you speak, and in the way you act. Include it in your application section as you summarize what you've learned from Ephesians 4.

Ephesians 4:1-16

Ephesians 4:17-32

Hashtag #:

One-Sentence Summary:

My Application(s):

WEEK EIGHT
Learning What Is Pleasing

". . . walk in love, just as Christ also loved you and gave
Himself up for us . . ."
–Ephesians 5:2

In Christ we are new creations, but we still need to learn to walk in that reality. In Christ we have everything that pertains to life and godliness, but we still need to take care how we walk. Deception doesn't sit down when you become a Christian. As long as we remain in a broken and fallen world, we need to be diligent to walk wisely in love as children of Light. Let's take a look!

Week Eight: **Learning What Is Pleasing**

REMEMBERING

Take a few minutes to summarize what you've learned so far.

WEEKLY READ-THROUGH #1

Version I read:

New observations/questions:

WEEKLY READ-THROUGH #2

Version I read:

New observations/questions:

WEEKLY READ-THROUGH #3

Version I read:

New observations/questions:

EPHESIANS 5:1-21

Paul continues to exhort his readers to live wisely what they are: beloved children, saints, children of Light.

OBSERVE the TEXT of SCRIPTURE

READ Ephesians 5:1-21 and **MARK** key words you notice.

Ephesians 5:1-21

1   *Therefore be imitators of God, as beloved children;*

2   *and walk in love, just as Christ also loved you and gave Himself up for us, an offering and a sacrifice to God as a fragrant aroma.*

3   *But immorality or any impurity or greed must not even be named among you, as is proper among saints;*

4   *and there must be no filthiness and silly talk, or coarse jesting, which are not fitting, but rather giving of thanks.*

5   *For this you know with certainty, that no immoral or impure person or covetous man, who is an idolater, has an inheritance in the kingdom of Christ and God.*

6   *Let no one deceive you with empty words, for because of these things the wrath of God comes upon the sons of disobedience.*

7   *Therefore do not be partakers with them;*

8   *for you were formerly darkness, but now you are Light in the Lord; walk as children of Light*

9   *(for the fruit of the Light consists in all goodness and righteousness and truth),*

10 *trying to learn what is pleasing to the Lord.*

11 *Do not participate in the unfruitful deeds of darkness, but instead even expose them;*

12 *for it is disgraceful even to speak of the things which are done by them in secret.*

GROW UP
Moving Past Spiritual Adolescence
EPHESIANS

Week Eight: **Learning What Is Pleasing**

13 But all things become visible when they are exposed by the light, for everything that becomes visible is light.

14 For this reason it says, "Awake, sleeper, and arise from the dead, and Christ will shine on you."

15 Therefore be careful how you walk, not as unwise men but as wise,

16 making the most of your time, because the days are evil.

17 So then do not be foolish, but understand what the will of the Lord is.

18 And do not get drunk with wine, for that is dissipation, but be filled with the Spirit,

19 speaking to one another in psalms and hymns and spiritual songs, singing and making melody with your heart to the Lord;

20 always giving thanks for all things in the name of our Lord Jesus Christ to God, even the Father;

21 and be subject to one another in the fear of Christ.

DISCUSS with your GROUP or PONDER on your own . . .

What did you initially observe from the text?

How does Ephesians 5:1 tie in with Paul's train of thought at the end of chapter 4?

What questions from your first read of Ephesians 5 do you hope to dig out answers for?

LOOKING EVEN CLOSER . . .

Although Ephesians 5 is 33 verses long, we're only going to cover verses 1-21 this week. We'll look at the remaining verses from Ephesians 5 next week along with Ephesians 6 since the content overlaps the two chapters.

OBSERVE the TEXT of SCRIPTURE

READ Ephesians 5:1-5 and **MARK** every reference to *God* and to *Christ*. **CIRCLE** everything Paul says his readers should do. **UNDERLINE** everything Paul says they shouldn't be or do.

Ephesians 5:1-5

1 Therefore be imitators of God, as beloved children;

2 and walk in love, just as Christ also loved you and gave Himself up for us, an offering and a sacrifice to God as a fragrant aroma.

3 But immorality or any impurity or greed must not even be named among you, as is proper among saints;

4 and there must be no filthiness and silly talk, or coarse jesting, which are not fitting, but rather giving of thanks.

5 For this you know with certainty, that no immoral or impure person or covetous man, who is an idolater, has an inheritance in the kingdom of Christ and God.

DISCUSS with your GROUP or PONDER on your own . . .

Who are we to imitate and why?

Paul has already said that we are to walk in good works (2:10) and walk worthy of our calling (4:1). What else does he add in verse 2 and how do you think it is related?

How did Christ's behavior show His love? How does this compare with common cultural definitions of love?

ONE STEP FURTHER:

Walking . . .

If you have extra time this week, see what Paul and other biblical writers have to say about how believers should walk. Then record below what you discover.

GROW UP
Moving Past Spiritual Adolescence
EPHESIANS

What does walking in love "just as Christ also loved you" involve? What's an example from your life?

What terms does Paul use to describe readers in this section?

According to verse 3 what does Paul say should "not even be named" among saints? Why? What does it have to do with how he defines them?

How common do you think these bad attitudes and behaviors are today in the world? In our churches?

What else should saints not be doing according to verse 4? Does Paul have a particular category of sin in mind?

What are some examples of these sins? How common do you think they are today? Why?

Digging Deeper

Hebrews 10 and Sacrifices

Since Christ gave Himself up for us as "an offering and a sacrifice to God," take some time this week to read carefully through Hebrews 10 to see what you can learn about sacrifices and offerings. I'll give you some questions to get you started but dig as deeply as you want both here and elsewhere in the Word!

What were the sacrifices offered under the Law unable to do?

How often were they offered?

How did the offering of Jesus differ? What did it accomplish?

How did Jesus' offering change the believer's approach to God?

How did it change the believer's ability to obey God? Explain.

Week Eight: **Learning What Is Pleasing**

What should saints be doing with their mouths instead?

What does Paul say his readers can know for sure?

Do you think there are immoral, impure, and covetous people today who think they have a relationship with Christ? Given the opportunity, how would you explain Ephesians 5 to them?

OBSERVE the TEXT of SCRIPTURE

READ Ephesians 5:6-14 and **MARK** every reference to *darkness*. Also **MARK** every reference to *Light*.

Ephesians 5:6-14

6 *Let no one deceive you with empty words, for because of these things the wrath of God comes upon the sons of disobedience.*

7 *Therefore do not be partakers with them;*

8 *for you were formerly darkness, but now you are Light in the Lord; walk as children of Light*

9 *(for the fruit of the Light consists in all goodness and righteousness and truth),*

10 *trying to learn what is pleasing to the Lord.*

11 *Do not participate in the unfruitful deeds of darkness, but instead even expose them;*

12 *for it is disgraceful even to speak of the things which are done by them in secret.*

13 *But all things become visible when they are exposed by the light, for everything that becomes visible is light.*

14 *For this reason it says, "Awake, sleeper, and arise from the dead, and Christ will shine on you."*

DISCUSS with your GROUP or PONDER on your own . . .

What does Paul warn against in verse 6? What is the specific threat? Where do we see evidences of "these things" today?

While Paul spoke of Christ's love in verse 2, what does he discuss about God in verse 6? Who needs to be concerned and why?

What specifically are "these things" that invite the wrath of God? How does verse 6 connect with the previous verses?

Using the Bible, how would you explain the co-existence of the love of God and the wrath of God to an unbeliever or a new believer?

Very simply, what does Paul tell his readers to avoid? What does this have to do with what they were in comparison to what they are?

According to verse 8, how does Paul say his readers should walk and why?

FYI:

Shine!

"Let your light shine before men in such a way that they may see your good works, and glorify your Father who is in heaven."

—Jesus, Matthew 5:16

GROW UP

Moving Past Spiritual Adolescence
EPHESIANS

Week Eight: **Learning What Is Pleasing**

What does Paul say about the fruit of the Light?

ONE STEP FURTHER:

Word Study: Pleasing
Take some time to find the Greek word that is translated "pleasing." Then see where and how it is used throughout the New Testament. Record your findings below.

How can we learn what is pleasing to the Lord? Support your answer from Scripture.

How does Paul describe the deeds of darkness in verse 11? How does this contrast with the Light?

What should those who are "Light in the Lord" do and not do when they encounter the deeds of darkness?

What disgraceful action does Paul describe in verse 12? Do you ever do this and rationalize it? If so, how do you rationalize?

What effect does light have on dark deeds?

How are you responding to verse 14's call?

OBSERVE the TEXT of SCRIPTURE

READ Ephesians 5:15-21 and **MARK** every reference to *wise*. Also **MARK** all references to *foolish/unwise*.

Ephesians 5:15-21

15 Therefore be careful how you walk, not as unwise men but as wise,

16 making the most of your time, because the days are evil.

17 So then do not be foolish, but understand what the will of the Lord is.

18 And do not get drunk with wine, for that is dissipation, but be filled with the Spirit,

19 speaking to one another in psalms and hymns and spiritual songs, singing and making melody with your heart to the Lord;

20 always giving thanks for all things in the name of our Lord Jesus Christ to God, even the Father;

21 and be subject to one another in the fear of Christ.

DISCUSS with your GROUP or PONDER on your own . . .

What additional walking instructions does Paul give in verse 15 and why?

"Be careful" translates two Greek words *blepo* ("see" or "look") and *akribos* ("diligently" or "accurately"). How do we do this in our walk today? How can our vision be distorted?

GROW UP

Moving Past Spiritual Adolescence
EPHESIANS

FYI:

Teach Us!

So teach us to number our days, that we may present to You a heart of wisdom.

—Psalm 90:12

Week Eight: **Learning What Is Pleasing**

What does "time" have to do with walking wisely? How are you doing at managing this limited resource?

What characterized "the days" Paul was writing? How would you characterize our days?

What is set in opposition to "foolish" in verse 17?

What have we learned about "the will of the Lord" so far in Ephesians?

What conditions does Paul begin to contrast in verse 18? How does he further describe each?

What characterizes the speech of those who are filled with the Spirit?

GROW UP
Moving Past Spiritual Adolescence
EPHESIANS

How do people filled with the Spirit interact with one another? Is this typical of your interactions with fellow believers? If not, what changes do you need to make?

How are you subjecting yourself to others in the fear of Christ?

@THE END OF THE DAY . . .

Take some time to reflect on what you learned this week and consider how it fits in with what you learned earlier. What have you learned that will change the way you think and act?

Ephesians 1

Ephesians 2

Ephesians 3

Ephesians 4

Ephesians 5:1-20

Hashtag #:

One-Sentence Summary:

My Application(s):

GROW UP
Moving Past Spiritual Adolescence
EPHESIANS

Week Eight: **Learning What Is Pleasing**

WEEK NINE
Subject to One Another

"and be subject to one another in the fear of Christ."
–Ephesians 5:21

To a culture that exalts power and desires control as much as it does cold hard cash, the command to "be subject" is not an easy sell. And while we bristle at it from our place in history, the teaching was *even more* disruptive in its original cultural context as Paul addressed believers across diverse social strata and called them *all* to selfless living for the benefit of the body of Christ.

Week Nine: **Subject to One Another**

REMEMBERING

Take a few minutes to summarize the main points in Ephesians 1–4.

Briefly summarize Ephesians 5:1-20.

WEEKLY READ-THROUGH #1

Version I read:

New observations/questions:

WEEKLY READ-THROUGH #2

Version I read:

New observations/questions:

WEEKLY READ-THROUGH #3

Version I read:

New observations/questions:

EPHESIANS 5 and 6

Since the apostle's inspired train of thought crosses over the Bible's uninspired chapter breaks, we're going to stick with Paul as he records God's Word about proper relationships.

OBSERVE the TEXT of SCRIPTURE

READ Ephesians 5:21–6:9 and **MARK** any key words that stand out.

Ephesians 5:21–6:9

21 *and be subject to one another in the fear of Christ.*

22 *Wives, be subject to your own husbands, as to the Lord.*

23 *For the husband is the head of the wife, as Christ also is the head of the church, He Himself being the Savior of the body.*

24 *But as the church is subject to Christ, so also the wives ought to be to their husbands in everything.*

25 *Husbands, love your wives, just as Christ also loved the church and gave Himself up for her,*

26 *so that He might sanctify her, having cleansed her by the washing of water with the word,*

27 *that He might present to Himself the church in all her glory, having no spot or wrinkle or any such thing; but that she would be holy and blameless.*

28 *So husbands ought also to love their own wives as their own bodies. He who loves his own wife loves himself;*

29 *for no one ever hated his own flesh, but nourishes and cherishes it, just as Christ also does the church,*

30 *because we are members of His body.*

31 *FOR THIS REASON A MAN SHALL LEAVE HIS FATHER AND MOTHER AND SHALL BE JOINED TO HIS WIFE, AND THE TWO SHALL BECOME ONE FLESH.*

Week Nine: **Subject to One Another**

32 This mystery is great; but I am speaking with reference to Christ and the church.

33 Nevertheless, each individual among you also is to love his own wife even as himself, and the wife must see to it that she respects her husband.

Ephesians 6

1 Children, obey your parents in the Lord, for this is right.

2 HONOR YOUR FATHER AND MOTHER (which is the first commandment with a promise),

3 SO THAT IT MAY BE WELL WITH YOU, AND THAT YOU MAY LIVE LONG ON THE EARTH.

4 Fathers, do not provoke your children to anger, but bring them up in the discipline and instruction of the Lord.

5 Slaves, be obedient to those who are your masters according to the flesh, with fear and trembling, in the sincerity of your heart, as to Christ;

6 not by way of eyeservice, as men-pleasers, but as slaves of Christ, doing the will of God from the heart.

7 With good will render service, as to the Lord, and not to men,

8 knowing that whatever good thing each one does, this he will receive back from the Lord, whether slave or free.

9 And masters, do the same things to them, and give up threatening, knowing that both their Master and yours is in heaven, and there is no partiality with Him.

DISCUSS with your GROUP or PONDER on your own . . .

What did you initially observe from the text?

How does this tie in with the first half of Ephesians 5?

GROW UP
Moving Past Spiritual Adolescence
EPHESIANS

What questions do you want answered?

ONE STEP FURTHER:

Word Study: Fear
The Greek root for fear [*phob*] is found twice in our passage, first as a noun (v. 21) then as a verb (v. 33). How is it translated in verse 33?

Paul uses the noun again in 6:5 and that's it for Ephesians. Now explore where and how the word is used throughout the rest of Paul's writings and the New Testament. Once you've done your research, explain how you think Paul is using the word "fear" in this context.

OBSERVE the TEXT of SCRIPTURE

READ Ephesians 5:21-33 and **MARK** in a distinct way every reference to *wives* and *husbands*, every reference to *Christ/Lord* and *the church*, and every reference to the verb *be subject*.

Ephesians 5:21-33

21 and be subject to one another in the fear of Christ.

22 Wives, be subject *to your own husbands, as to the Lord.*

23 For the husband is the head of the wife, as Christ also is the head of the church, He Himself being the Savior of the body.

24 But as the church is subject to Christ, so also the wives ought to be *to their husbands in everything.*

25 Husbands, love your wives, just as Christ also loved the church and gave Himself up for her,

26 so that He might sanctify her, having cleansed her by the washing of water with the word,

27 that He might present to Himself the church in all her glory, having no spot or wrinkle or any such thing; but that she would be holy and blameless.

28 So husbands ought also to love their own wives as their own bodies. He who loves his own wife loves himself;

29 for no one ever hated his own flesh, but nourishes and cherishes it, just as Christ also does the church,

30 because we are members of His body.

31 FOR THIS REASON A MAN SHALL LEAVE HIS FATHER AND MOTHER AND SHALL BE JOINED TO HIS WIFE, AND THE TWO SHALL BECOME ONE FLESH.

32 This mystery is great; but I am speaking with reference to Christ and the church.

33 Nevertheless, each individual among you also is to love his own wife even as himself, and the wife must see to it *that she respects her husband.*

GROW UP
Moving Past Spiritual Adolescence
EPHESIANS

DISCUSS with your GROUP or PONDER on your own . . .

What is the overriding command of this section?

FYI:

The First Marriage

18 Then the LORD God said, "It is not good for the man to be alone; I will make him a helper suitable for him."

19 Out of the ground the LORD God formed every beast of the field and every bird of the sky, and brought them to the man to see what he would call them; and whatever the man called a living creature, that was its name.

20 The man gave names to all the cattle, and to the birds of the sky, and to every beast of the field, but for Adam there was not found a helper suitable for him.

21 So the LORD God caused a deep sleep to fall upon the man, and he slept; then He took one of his ribs and closed up the flesh at that place.

22 The LORD God fashioned into a woman the rib which He had taken from the man, and brought her to the man.

23 The man said,

> *"This is now bone of my bones,*
> *And flesh of my flesh;*
> *She shall be called Woman,*
> *Because she was taken out of Man."*

24 For this reason a man shall leave his father and his mother, and be joined to his wife; and they shall become one flesh.

25 And the man and his wife were both naked and were not ashamed.

> —Genesis 2:18-25

What relationship does Paul talk about in verses 22-33 and what other relationship does it picture?

What does Paul command the wives in verses 22-24? Why?

Does this apply to women and men in general? Why or why not? Why does this matter?

What does Paul command the husbands in verse 25? Who is the example in this and what did He do? (You might want to make a list!!)

How and why are husbands to love their wives? What actions are associated with the verb "love" (Greek: *agapao*)?

GROW UP

Moving Past Spiritual Adolescence
EPHESIANS

If a husband doesn't love his wife, what logical affect will this have on him? Why?

What is the great mystery that Paul is talking about here, and how does it relate to husbands and wives? How does it relate to what we've seen so far in Ephesians?

What is Paul's final summary of husband-and-wife responsibilities in verse 33? How are they reciprocal? Which do you think is harder? What if your obedience to these verses is not reciprocated by the other party? Read 1 Peter 2:18–3:9.

If you are a wife, what are some ways you can respect your husband today? If you are a husband, what are some ways you can love your wife today?

Again, if you are a wife, are there any ways you habitually disrespect your husband? If you are a husband, are there any areas in which you habitually fail to love your wife? If so, write them down and ask God to lead you to new behaviors that honor both Him and your spouse.

Week Nine: **Subject to One Another**

OBSERVE the TEXT of SCRIPTURE

READ Ephesians 6:1-4 and **MARK** in a distinct way every reference to *children* and *parents* (include *mother* and *father*) and every reference to the *Lord*.

Ephesians 6:1-4

1   *Children, obey your parents in the Lord, for this is right.*

2   *HONOR YOUR FATHER AND MOTHER (which is the first commandment with a promise),*

3   *SO THAT IT MAY BE WELL WITH YOU, AND THAT YOU MAY LIVE LONG ON THE EARTH.*

4   *Fathers, do not provoke your children to anger, but bring them up in the discipline and instruction of the Lord.*

DISCUSS with your GROUP or PONDER on your own . . .

Summarize Paul's relationship commands so far. What is the overriding command to all? The command to wives? The command to husbands?

Now, what does he command children to do and why?

How long do you think each of these applies? Answer and explain by reasoning through the greater context of this passage and other applicable scriptures.

FYI:

Number Five

Honor your father and your mother, that your days may be prolonged in the land which the LORD your God gives you.

—Exodus 20:12

What are some ways adult children can honor parents?

What corresponding command does Paul give to "fathers"? How do the commands to children and fathers work together?

How do you think people today are doing at bringing up children in the discipline and instruction of the Lord? How does the culture at large impact this?

If you have kids or grandkids, how are you doing? Where do you see room for improvement?

Is it okay to provoke your children if they provoke you first? Okay. Just had to ask. Moving on . . . ☺

ONE STEP FURTHER:

Word Study: Provoke
What does *provoke to anger* mean? Find the Greek word Paul uses and see what you can discover about it this week. Then record your findings and applications below.

GROW UP
Moving Past Spiritual Adolescence
EPHESIANS

OBSERVE the TEXT of SCRIPTURE

READ Ephesians 6:5-9 and **MARK** in a distinct way every reference to *slaves* and *masters*, and every reference to the *Lord/Christ*.

Ephesians 6:5-9

5 *Slaves, be obedient to those who are your masters according to the flesh, with fear and trembling, in the sincerity of your heart, as to Christ;*

6 *not by way of eyeservice, as men-pleasers, but as slaves of Christ, doing the will of God from the heart.*

7 *With good will render service, as to the Lord, and not to men,*

8 *knowing that whatever good thing each one does, this he will receive back from the Lord, whether slave or free.*

9 *And masters, do the same things to them, and give up threatening, knowing that both their Master and yours is in heaven, and there is no partiality with Him.*

DISCUSS with your GROUP or PONDER on your own . . .

Who does Paul address in verse 5? How does he qualify the address?

What's a modern-day application of the principle?

How should slaves relate to their masters?

What core heart issues does Paul go after with this group of people?

ONE STEP FURTHER:

Word Studies!!!

There is so much good stuff to dig at in this section—don't miss out! Pick a couple of the words below to explore further and have a blast using blueletterbible.org or your favorite word study tool(s)!

Sincerity

Eyeservice

Men-pleasers

Threatening

Partiality

How do you think your work relationships would change if you continually remembered that God is your ultimate boss?

What hope does this give you if you have a difficult boss?

What are some ways we give in to eyeservice and people-pleasing in our cultural context?

What radical commands does Paul speak to earthly masters? How would these have been countercultural in his day?

Do you think demands on "masters" are still countercultural? Why/why not?

What role does "threatening" play in our culture in business and elsewhere? In what way can you, as a follower of Christ, lead without threats, veiled or otherwise?

> **FYI:**
>
> **New Testament Slavery**
>
> Let's be clear, what Paul talks about as slavery is not what first pops into the minds of most people today. For most of us, our minds jump to racial slavery in the United States' antebellum South or to human trafficking around the world today.
>
> In New Testament times there certainly were forms of slavery that were not acceptable—those that came about due to kidnapping and other nefarious means—but more often slavery was an enforced service to repay a personal or societal debt. The closest parallel we have today is a court-ordered penalty for duties specified by contract but defaulted on.

GROW UP
Moving Past Spiritual Adolescence
EPHESIANS

Week Nine: **Subject to One Another**

Digging Deeper

Submission and Humility in the Life of Jesus

If you have some extra time this week, invest some of it in exploring how Jesus modeled the right relationships He calls His followers to in Ephesians. As you pursue this open-ended opportunity, remember to investigate His relationship with the Father, with His disciples, and with others He interacted with. You'll also want to make sure to do a thorough word study on *hupotasso* ("subject"). Have fun!!

@THE END OF THE DAY . . .

Steel wool; that's what certain passages of Scripture are to me. Ephesians 5 is one of those. If it's the same for you, I'd encourage you to read back through the texts you've studied and ask God to help you understand how to radically obey in one specific area. Sound good? Remember, He is a gentle Shepherd who loves you more than you'll ever comprehend. Again, take time to record what you remember from previous chapters as you consider God's instructions and commands in Ephesians 5:21–6:9.

Ephesians 1

Ephesians 2

Ephesians 3

Ephesians 4

Ephesians 5:1-20

Ephesians 5:21–6:9

Hashtag #:

One-Sentence Summary:

My Application(s):

GROW UP
Moving Past Spiritual Adolescence
EPHESIANS

Week Nine: **Subject to One Another**

WEEK TEN
Resist! Stand Firm!

"Therefore, take up the full armor of God, so that you will be able to resist in the evil day, and having done everything, to stand firm."
–Ephesians 6:13

We're in a war, but we do not battle alone or from weakness! Paul's final call to the Ephesians—the one new man in Christ, made up of Jewish and Gentile believers—is "stand firm" in God's strength together. While Ephesians 6:10-17 is often peeled out of the context of the letter to teach about spiritual warfare, doing so dilutes the impact of the message which is built on the foundational truths of Christ's victory over sin and death and His current position in the heavenly places "far above all rule and authority and power and dominion, and every name that is named" (Ephesians 1:21). Let's get at it!

Week Ten: **Resist! Stand Firm!**

REMEMBERING

Let's review. As simply and concisely as possible, summarize the letter to the Ephesians chapter by chapter. As you do this, take into account the main theological points and do your best to make them easy *for you* to recall. Ask yourself on each answer, "Will I remember this point next year?" If the answer is "No," give it another shot.

Ephesians 1

Ephesians 2

Ephesians 3

Ephesians 4

Ephesians 5

Ephesians 6a

WEEKLY READ-THROUGH #1

Version I read:

New observations/questions:

WEEKLY READ-THROUGH #2

Version I read:

New observations/questions:

Week Ten: **Resist! Stand Firm!**

WEEKLY READ-THROUGH #3

Version I read:

New observations/questions:

What was your favorite translation to read and why?

OBSERVE the TEXT of SCRIPTURE

READ Ephesians 6:10-24 and **MARK** any key words that stand out.

Ephesians 6:10-24

10 *Finally, be strong in the Lord and in the strength of His might.*

11 *Put on the full armor of God, so that you will be able to stand firm against the schemes of the devil.*

12 *For our struggle is not against flesh and blood, but against the rulers, against the powers, against the world forces of this darkness, against the spiritual* forces *of wickedness in the heavenly* places.

13 *Therefore, take up the full armor of God, so that you will be able to resist in the evil day, and having done everything, to stand firm.*

14 *Stand firm therefore, HAVING GIRDED YOUR LOINS WITH TRUTH, and HAVING PUT ON THE BREASTPLATE OF RIGHTEOUSNESS,*

15 *and having shod YOUR FEET WITH THE PREPARATION OF THE GOSPEL OF PEACE;*

16 *in addition to all, taking up the shield of faith with which you will be able to extinguish all the flaming arrows of the evil* one.

17 *And take THE HELMET OF SALVATION, and the sword of the Spirit, which is the word of God.*

18 With all prayer and petition pray at all times in the Spirit, and with this in view, be on the alert with all perseverance and petition for all the saints,

19 and pray on my behalf, that utterance may be given to me in the opening of my mouth, to make known with boldness the mystery of the gospel,

20 for which I am an ambassador in chains; that in proclaiming it I may speak boldly, as I ought to speak.

21 But that you also may know about my circumstances, how I am doing, Tychicus, the beloved brother and faithful minister in the Lord, will make everything known to you.

22 I have sent him to you for this very purpose, so that you may know about us, and that he may comfort your hearts.

23 Peace be to the brethren, and love with faith, from God the Father and the Lord Jesus Christ.

24 Grace be with all those who love our Lord Jesus Christ with incorruptible love.

DISCUSS with your GROUP or PONDER on your own . . .

What did you initially observe from the text?

How does this section function in relation to the rest of the letter?

What questions do you want answered?

OBSERVE the TEXT of SCRIPTURE

READ Ephesians 6:10-12 and compare with Ephesians 1:18-23.

MARK the phrase *strength of His might* in both passages.

MARK the phrases *be strong* and *will be able* in Ephesians 6:10-12 and *power* in Ephesians 1:18-23. (Note: All of these words are from the Greek root *dunamis*.)

MARK the phrase *stand firm* in Ephesians 6:10-12. (We'll keep marking this one in the next section!)

Finally, **MARK** the phrase *in the heavenly places* in both passages.

Ephesians 6:10-12

10 *Finally, be strong in the Lord and in the strength of His might.*

11 *Put on the full armor of God, so that you will be able to stand firm against the schemes of the devil.*

12 *For our struggle is not against flesh and blood, but against the rulers, against the powers, against the world forces of this darkness, against the spiritual forces of wickedness in the heavenly places.*

Ephesians 1:18-23

18 *I pray that the eyes of your heart may be enlightened, so that you will know what is the hope of His calling, what are the riches of the glory of His inheritance in the saints,*

19 *and what is the surpassing greatness of His power toward us who believe. These are in accordance with the working of the strength of His might*

20 *which He brought about in Christ, when He raised Him from the dead and seated Him at His right hand in the heavenly places,*

21 *far above all rule and authority and power and dominion, and every name that is named, not only in this age but also in the one to come.*

22 *And He put all things in subjection under His feet, and gave Him as head over all things to the church,*

23 *which is His body, the fullness of Him who fills all in all.*

DISCUSS with your GROUP or PONDER on your own . . .

What does Paul command the Ephesians to do in 6:10? What is the source?

FYI:

Be Strong

When Paul says "be strong" in Ephesians 6:10, he uses a second person plural passive. Passive voices ordinarily switch subjects: here, since the strengthener is God ("His might"), the statement seems more like a benediction (blessing) than a command to be obeyed like "Go strengthen yourself!"

Being strengthened *by God's power* is the key, not your resolve to strengthen yourself. In southern English in the US the construction would be better translated, "Finally, all y'all be strengthened in the Lord." The northern equivalent that takes into account both the passive and the plural would be, "Finally, all you guys be strengthened in the Lord." We are not strong on our own, we are strong together in the strength of the Lord.

GROW UP
Moving Past Spiritual Adolescence
EPHESIANS

Looking at both passages, what do we learn about the phrase "the strength of His might"? What does it have to do with the ability of Christians to "be strong"? Where has the strength of God's might been most clearly revealed?

What does Paul tell the Ephesians to do so they will have the power to stand firm? Why will we need this?

What are Christians standing against? What do we learn about our enemy?

What are some of the schemes of the devil that we have seen demonstrated in the letter to the Ephesians? Elsewhere in Scripture?

How does being aware of particular schemes help you stand against them? Do you recognize what he has used against you? Explain.

Are you struggling successfully against the devil's schemes or is he "pinning" you? Explain.

ONE STEP FURTHER:

Our Spiritual Opponents
If you have extra time, see what you can learn about what Christians struggle against according to Ephesians 6:12:

rulers

powers

world forces of this darkness

spiritual forces of wickedness

Summarize below what you learned about our spiritual opponents as a whole:

GROW UP
Moving Past Spiritual Adolescence
EPHESIANS

Week Ten: **Resist! Stand Firm!**

What is the Christian struggle against? What is it *not* against? What difference does this make?

Finally, how does Christ's being in "the heavenly places" (Ephesians 1) help us interpret and apply what we read about "the heavenly places" in Ephesians 6?

Why can Christians confidently go into spiritual "hand-to-hand" combat?

How do these truths encourage you? How can you use them to encourage others?

OBSERVE the TEXT of SCRIPTURE

READ Ephesians 6:13-17 and **MARK** in the same way the phrase *stand firm* and the word *resist*. **UNDERLINE** each piece of the armor of God.

Ephesians 6:13-17

13 *Therefore, take up the full armor of God, so that you will be able to resist in the evil day, and having done everything, to stand firm.*

14 *Stand firm therefore, HAVING GIRDED YOUR LOINS WITH TRUTH, and HAVING PUT ON THE BREASTPLATE OF RIGHTEOUSNESS,*

15 *and having shod YOUR FEET WITH THE PREPARATION OF THE GOSPEL OF PEACE;*

16 *in addition to all, taking up the shield of faith with which you will be able to extinguish all the flaming arrows of the evil one.*

17 *And take THE HELMET OF SALVATION, and the sword of the Spirit, which is the word of God.*

FYI:

Full Armor
"Full armor" translates the Greek compound word *panoplia* which means "all," "whole," or "every" (*pan*) "weapon" (*hoplon*).

GROW UP
Moving Past Spiritual Adolescence
EPHESIANS

DISCUSS with your GROUP or PONDER on your own . . .

How does verse 13 compare with Paul's previous command in verse 11? How do you think verse 12 relates to them?

Do you think "the evil day" applies to the times we are living in? Why/why not? Consider Ephesians 5:16 when you answer.

While we are strengthened by the Lord in His strength, what responsibility do we have in battle?`

What pieces of armor are we to wear? What does each protect or do? (This would be a great place to make a list!)

Armor	Purpose

ONE STEP FURTHER:

Word Study: Stand Firm

If you have time this week, find the Greek word that is translated "stand firm" and see what other word in this section it is related to and how. Then explore the rest of the New Testament to see how this word is used, particularly in the Epistles. Record your findings below.

GROW UP
Moving Past Spiritual Adolescence
EPHESIANS

Week Ten: **Resist! Stand Firm!**

Let's take a look at a couple of cross-references to see what more we can discover about this armor. Whose armor do Isaiah 11:4-5 and 59:17 describe? How does this armor become our armor?

What roles do truth and righteousness play in your day-to-day life? Do you bear the image of Christ?

What about your understanding of the Gospel? Do you understand it well enough to share it with others?

Why does Paul say we need a shield? What is that shield?

Reflect for a moment on your daily life. Are you surprised by attacks, by "flaming arrows of the evil one"? Should you be? When they come, how can you stand firm? Where can you find examples of others who did?

What piece of armor protects the head? If you know Christ and know you have salvation in Him, how will this change the way you live?

What is the Christian's one offensive weapon? Are you well enough trained to wield it? Explain.

How can you improve in this area?

Briefly explain how the different parts of the armor of God work together.

OBSERVE the TEXT of SCRIPTURE

READ Ephesians 6:18-24 and **UNDERLINE** Paul's final instructions to the Ephesians.

Ephesians 6:18-24

18 *With all prayer and petition pray at all times in the Spirit, and with this in view, be on the alert with all perseverance and petition for all the saints,*

19 *and pray on my behalf, that utterance may be given to me in the opening of my mouth, to make known with boldness the mystery of the gospel,*

20 *for which I am an ambassador in chains; that in proclaiming it I may speak boldly, as I ought to speak.*

21 *But that you also may know about my circumstances, how I am doing, Tychicus, the beloved brother and faithful minister in the Lord, will make everything known to you.*

22 *I have sent him to you for this very purpose, so that you may know about us, and that he may comfort your hearts.*

23 *Peace be to the brethren, and love with faith, from God the Father and the Lord Jesus Christ.*

24 *Grace be with all those who love our Lord Jesus Christ with incorruptible love.*

DISCUSS with your GROUP or PONDER on your own . . .

What does Paul tell believers to do in verse 18? When and how should they do them?

What specific prayer requests does Paul make for himself in verses 19 and 20? Does that surprise you? Why/why not?

Who is Tychicus and what does Paul say about him?

How would you compare Paul's circumstances at the end of this letter with his heart for his readers?

Finally, how does Paul describe the love of Christians for Jesus? How is *your* love for Him today? What effect does this have on everything else?

@THE END OF THE DAY . . .

Let's summarize our final section of text before considering key takeaways from the entire letter.

Ephesians 6:10-24

Hashtag #:

One-Sentence Summary:

My Application(s):

Now, take time to page back through Paul's letter to the Ephesians and reflect on what God has taught you. Spend some time praying and asking Him to reveal to you what truth from His Word you most need to focus on at this point in your life and how you can go about applying it daily. Take as much time and as much space on the paper as you need to process, but then try to consolidate that truth into one sentence and write down what part of Ephesians it comes from. In remembering, sometimes less is more. Write that truth down on paper and ask God to engrave it on your heart as you seek to live a life pleasing to Him!

GROW UP
Moving Past Spiritual Adolescence
EPHESIANS

RESOURCES

Helpful Study Tools

How to Study Your Bible
Eugene, Oregon: Harvest House
Publishers

The New Inductive Study Bible
Eugene, Oregon: Harvest House
Publishers

Logos Bible Software
Available at www.logos.com.

Greek Word Study Tools

Kittel, G., Friedrich, G., & Bromiley,
G.W.
*Theological Dictionary of the New
Testament, Abridged* (also known as
Little Kittel)
Grand Rapids, Michigan: W.B.
Eerdmans Publishing Company

Hebrew Word Study Tools

Harris, R.L., Archer, G.L., & Walker,
B.K.
*Theological Wordbook of the Old
Testament* (also known as TWOT)
Chicago, Illinois: Moody Press

General Word Study Tools

Strong, James
*The New Strong's Exhaustive
Concordance of the Bible*
Nashville, Tennessee: Thomas Nelson

Recommended Commentary Sets

Expositor's Bible Commentary
Grand Rapids, Michigan: Zondervan

NIV Application Commentary
Grand Rapids, Michigan: Zondervan

The New American Commentary
Nashville, Tennessee: Broadman and
Holman Publishers

One-Volume Commentary

Carson, D.A., France, R.T., Motyer,
J.A., & Wenham, G.J. Ed.
*New Bible Commentary: 21st Century
Edition*
Downers Grove, Illinois: Inter-Varsity
Press

Rydelnik, M.,.Vanlaningham, M., Ed.
The Moody Bible Commentary
Chicago, Illinois: Moody Publishers

HOW TO DO AN ONLINE WORD STUDY

For use with www.blueletterbible.org

1. Type in Bible verse. Change the version to NASB. Click the "Search" button.

2. When you arrive at the next screen, you will see a "Tools" button to the left of your verse .

3. Hover over the "Tools" button and select the "Interlinear" option to take you to the concordance link.

3. Click on the Strong's number which is the link to the original word in Greek or Hebrew.

Clicking this number will bring up another screen that will give you a brief definition of the word as well as list every occurrence of the Greek word in the New Testament or Hebrew word in the Old Testament. Before running to the dictionary definition, scan places where this word is used in Scripture and examine the general contexts where it is used.

ABOUT PRECEPT

Precept Ministries International was raised up by God for the sole purpose of establishing people in God's Word to produce reverence for Him. It serves as an arm of the church without respect to denomination. God has enabled Precept to reach across denominational lines without compromising the truths of His inerrant Word. We believe every word of the Bible was inspired and given to man as all that is necessary for him to become mature and thoroughly equipped for every good work of life. This ministry does not seek to impose its doctrines on others, but rather to direct people to the Master Himself, who leads and guides by His Spirit into all truth through a systematic study of His Word. The ministry produces a variety of Bible studies and holds conferences and intensive Training Workshops designed to establish attendees in the Word through Inductive Bible Study.

Jack Arthur and his wife, Kay, founded Precept Ministries in 1970. Kay and the ministry staff of writers produce **Precept Upon Precept**® studies, **In & Out**® studies, **Lord** series studies, the **New Inductive Study Series** studies, **40-Minute** studies, and **Discover 4 Yourself**® **Inductive Bible Studies for Kids**. Visit Shop.Precept.org to purchase these and many other Inductive Bible Studies. From years of diligent study and teaching experience, Kay and the staff have developed these unique, inductive courses that are now used in nearly 185 countries and 70 languages.

 PRECEPT.ORG

PAM GILLASPIE

Pam Gillaspie, a passionate Bible student and teacher, authors Precept's *Sweeter Than Chocolate!*® and *Cookies on the Lower Shelf*™ Bible study series. Pam holds a BA in Biblical Studies from Wheaton College in Wheaton, Illinois. She and her husband live in suburban Chicago, Illinois, with their daughter and Great Dane. They also have a married son and a new daughter-in-love. Pam's greatest joy is encouraging others to read God's Word widely and study it deeply . . . precept upon precept.

For speaking inquiries, questions, or just to connect, you can find Pam online at:

www.pamgillaspie.com

 pamgillaspie

 pamgillaspie

CPSIA information can be obtained
at www.ICGtesting.com
Printed in the USA
FFHW01n1933030818
47621555-51173FF

9 781621 196150